new directions
in indian dance

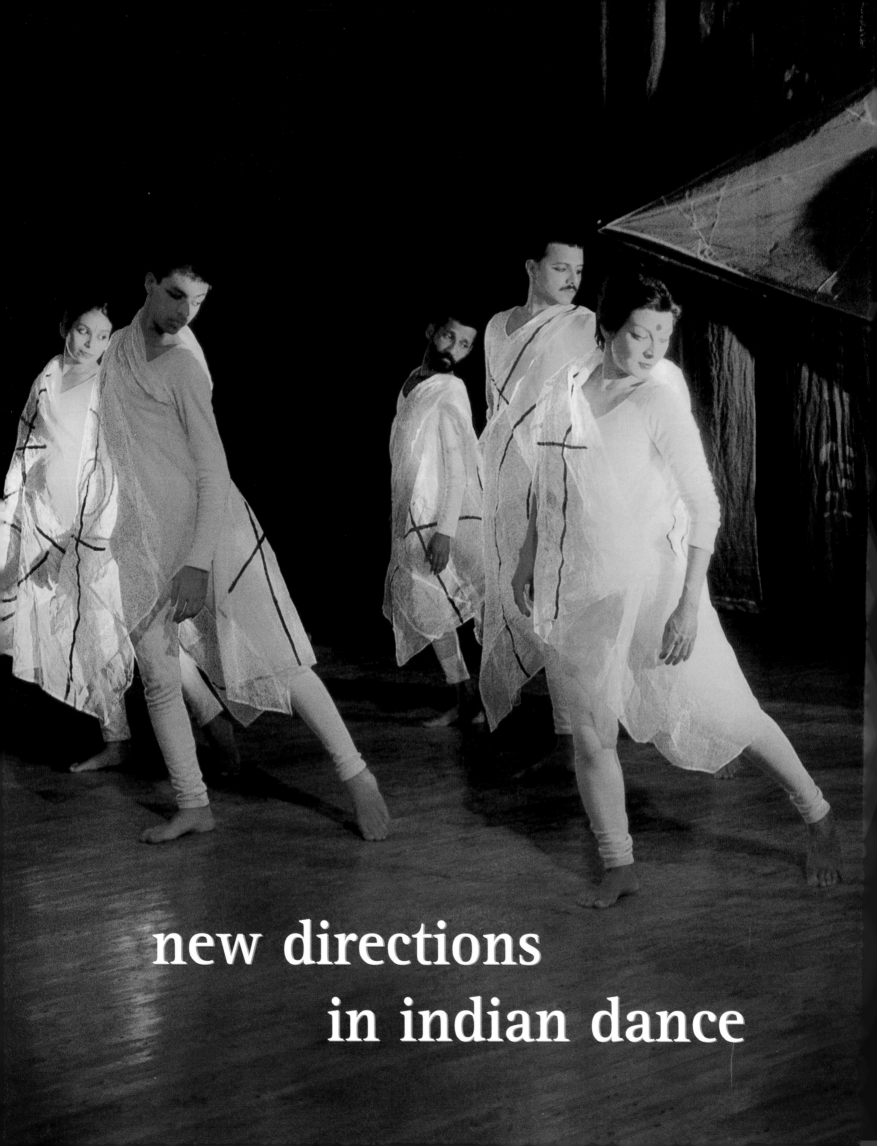

new directions
in indian dance

edited by Sunil Kothari

Marg

General Editor
PRATAPADITYA PAL
Research Editor
ANNAPURNA GARIMELLA

Executive Editors
SAVITA CHANDIRAMANI
RIVKA ISRAEL
Senior Editorial Executive
BISWAJEET RATH
Editorial Executives
ARNAVAZ K. BHANSALI
L.K. MEHTA

Designer
NAJU HIRANI
Senior Production Executive
GAUTAM V. JADHAV
Production Executive
VIDYADHAR R. SAWANT

Vol. 55 No. 2
December 2003
Reprint 2010
ISBN: 978-81-85026-62-6
Library of Congress Catalog
Card Number: 2003-306043

Published by Radhika Sabavala for
The Marg Foundation
at Army & Navy Building, 3rd Floor,
148, M.G. Road, Mumbai 400 001, India.
Processed at Reproscan, Mumbai 400 093.
Printed at Jak Printers Private Limited,
Mumbai 400 027, India.

Page 1: Astad Deboo in "Aahavan". Photograph: Neelesh Kale.
Pages 2–3: "Devi Mahatmya" by Mallika Sarabhai. Photograph:
Ashok Jani, courtesy Darpana Academy of Performing Arts, Ahmedabad.
Pages 4–5: Narendra Sharma's "Mukhantar". Photograph courtesy
Bhoomika Creative Dance Centre, New Delhi.
Pages 6–7: A dance sequence choreographed by Vaibhavi Merchant
for *Mumbai se Aaya Mera Dost* (2003). Photograph: John Panikar.

CONTENTS

8   Introduction
     Sunil Kothari

EARLY EXPERIMENTS

20   Modern Dance:
     The Contribution of Uday Shankar and
     His Associates
     Kapila Vatsyayan

32   Tagore and Modernization of Dance
     Manjusri Chaki Sircar

44   Traditional Dance and Contemporary
     Choreography
     Mrinalini Sarabhai

50   Reflections on New Directions in Indian Dance
     Chandralekha

INNOVATIONS IN SPECIFIC FORMS

60   Innovations in Kathak
     Kumudini Lakhia

70   Manipuri Dances:
     Extending the Boundaries
     Sunil Kothari

82   Navanritya – A Contemporary Methodology:
     History, Theory, Practice
     Ranjabati Sircar

PERSONAL EXPERIMENTS

94   Search for My Tongue
     Daksha Sheth

106   Re-membering "Wings of Shiva"
     Uttara Asha Coorlawala

118   Creating Endless Possibilities
     Astad Deboo

EXTENSIONS AT HOME AND ABROAD

132   Dance in Films
     Arundhathi Subramaniam

146   Explorations in Bharata Natyam Abroad
     Mamata Niyogi-Nakra

156   Growths and Outgrowths
     Sanjoy Roy

168   Reinscribing "Indian" Dance
     Uttara Asha Coorlawala

A CROSS-SECTION OF CHOREOGRAPHIC WORKS

177

202   Index

204   Contributors

The publication of this book has been
made possible by support received from the

SIR RATAN TATA TRUST
and

AHUJASONS SHAWL WALE (P) LTD.

ahujasons
Shawls • Stoles • Scarves

uction

Sunil Kothari

Perspective

Looking back on the dance scenario over the last fifty years in India, one is bound to ask such questions as: What is new in Indian dance? Are Indian dance traditions confined to classical dance? Is it possible to see something new, contemporary, modern, that reflects present-day themes in dance and in a language other than the familiar classical dance vocabularies?

In the late 1920s Indian dance made a mark on the national and international fronts. Through the efforts of pioneers like Uday Shankar, we rediscovered our heritage and reinvented various dance traditions. The form of dance that Uday Shankar created is today categorized as of a different genre, sometimes even called modern.

Indian classical dance did exist in the temples as a part of ritual worship and in the princely courts where dancers performed for patrons. As a reaction to British rule, the intelligentsia seeking a national identity revived the indigenous arts.

With this increasing awareness about Indian dance traditions, some of the pioneers founded institutions for training: Gurudev Rabindranath Tagore (1861–1941) introduced Manipuri and Kathakali in Santiniketan in the 1920s and '30s; poet Vallathol Narayana Menon established Kerala Kala Mandalam for Kathakali in Cheruturuthi in 1930; Rukmini Devi (1904–86) established Kalakshetra in Madras in 1936 essentially for Bharata Natyam; Uday Shankar (1900–77) established the Uday Shankar India Culture Centre at Almora in 1939; Madame Menaka (1899–1947) established Nrityalayam at Khandala, a hill station near Bombay in 1941, and also arranged for training in Kathak and other classical dance forms. These were people with modern sensibilities who had realized the importance and value of the dance traditions and why they should be preserved.

By the time India became independent, classical dance forms were firmly established and the number of dance students was growing. In 1954, with the establishment of the three academies Sangeet Natak Akademi, Lalit Kala Akademi, and Sahitya Akademi, the performing arts, plastic arts, and literature received support from the government of

1
Uday Shankar with Anna Pavlova in a Krishna-Radha work choreographed by Uday Shankar, staged at Covent Garden, London, 1923. Pavlova suggested Uday Shankar return to his roots and discover India's dance heritage. Photograph courtesy Sunil Kothari dance collection.

India. Institutions like the Indian Council for Cultural Relations provided opportunities for classical dance and music to be projected abroad under cultural agreements between India and other countries and in return received visiting dance and music troupes from abroad.

In the 1960s, '70s, and '80s, the popularity of classical dance forms reached its peak. The first All India Dance Seminar and Dance Festival in Delhi in 1958 brought to the fore two other classical dance forms, Odissi from Orissa and Kuchipudi from Andhra Pradesh. Mohini Attam, a solo dance form from Kerala practised by women was also recognized, and more recently, Sattriya of Assam has received recognition as the eighth classical dance form.

What is common to all these classical dances is that their roots are in religion, and mythological and devotional stories form their content. The expressional aspect tends to revolve around a *nayika*, the heroine, who pines for union with the *nayaka*, the hero. The heroine symbolizes the soul of a devotee, and the hero, the Lord, the super-soul with whom the soul wishes to unite. The spirit of the Bhakti movement, the cult of devotion, permeates these dance forms. But these themes led some to feel that the classical dance forms were fast turning into museum pieces.

Another factor which contributed to popular disinterest was an unprecedented growth in the number of dancers, some of whom were mediocre. Besides the assembly-line production of dancers, and the fact that performers now came from the middle class rather than the hereditary class, rampant commercialization also affected standards. To take the example of Bharata Natyam, while it has thrown up exceptionally gifted dancers, there has been a proliferation of pre-fabricated *arangetram*s and mechanical presentation. In urban centres, performances do not attract crowds and audiences are dwindling except for special events. However, one encounters a false hype and euphoria during, say, the December festival season in Chennai. Dancers who are sensitive to the gap between their own lives and what they perform on stage have questioned the relevance of a *nayika* eternally waiting for her *nayaka* and similar themes. The rapid shift in the background of the performers has led to an inevitable shift in the content of their dance too. However, a gifted dancer can still evoke bhakti or spirituality. Dancers with imagination and the ability to reflect upon our present existential crisis have deviated from the traditional *margam* (*alarippu* to *tillana*) repertoire. The narrative traditions in our culture coexist with the tradition of abstraction. Some dancers like Chandralekha have explored this area with more success, moving away from the *nayaka-nayika* themes.

The debate on where one would place the beginnings of modernism in Indian dance is as controversy-ridden as that which surrounds Western dance. Two events are possible contenders: the appearance of Uday Shankar in the 1920s, and the East-West Dance Encounter organized by Georg Lechner, the then Director of Max Mueller Bhavan, Bombay, in collaboration with the National Centre for the Performing Arts (NCPA) in Bombay in January 1984.

It is pertinent that Uday Shankar's legacy is followed by his close associate Narendra Sharma at his Bhoomika Creative Dance

Centre in New Delhi. In one of his recent productions "Antim Adhyay", his asceticism and understanding of art, without binding itself to any style but allowing the form to emerge from the issues, has succeeded in producing a free expressive dance theatre.

Another Uday Shankar disciple, the late Shanti Bardhan had, after parting company with him when he disbanded his company, created two major productions with originality: the "Ramayana" in which dancers performed like human puppets, and the "Panchatantra" where the movements were inspired by those of animals and birds.

In Calcutta, the relatives of Uday Shankar, his widow Amala Shankar, daughter Mamata Shankar, daughter-in-law Tanushree Shankar carry on his work. They attempt to keep alive the aesthetics of Uday Shankar's style. German critic Jochen Schmidt observed in *Ballet International* (July 1997) that those who have tried to create modern dance by melding Indian traditions with modern Western forms have invariably landed themselves in trouble. For somehow such attempts produce a mishmash and not modern dance.

The East-West Dance Encounter proved that many dancers who had seemed to be working in isolation, seeking new directions, were in fact in touch with other developments. The outcome of this conference was very rewarding. Contemporary dancers in the forefront who attended it included Mrinalini Sarabhai and her daughter Mallika Sarabhai, Kumudini Lakhia, Chandralekha, Yamini Krishnamurthy, Sonal Mansingh, Ritha Devi, Bharat Sharma, Sucheta Bhide, Chitra Sundaram, Uttara Asha Coorlawala, Astad Deboo, Avanthi Meduri, and others. Among the critics and scholars were Narayana Menon, Sadanand Menon, Shanta Serbjeet Singh, Shirin Vajifdar, connoisseur Jamshed Bhabha, painter Dashrath Patel, the legendary dancer Ram Gopal (1912–2003), and myself.

2
Gurudev Rabindranath Tagore, with young dancers in Santiniketan. Photograph: Viswabharati Archive, Santiniketan.

From the West came dancers/choreographers Susanne Linke and Gerhard Bohner from Germany, Dominique Bagouet, Andreine Bel, and Elizabeth Mauger from France, from England Stephen Long, trained at the Royal Ballet School, from Italy Patrizia Cerroni, from Canada Anne Marie Gaston, from the USA Carmen DeLavallade. There were two dancers settled in India: Sharon Lowen from the USA and Ileana Citaristi from Italy. Musician Igor Wakhevitch, a French citizen of Russian origin who had expressed interest in working with Indian dance, was also present.

Several issues were addressed and articulated and reports on these were published in the *NCPA Quarterly* (Vol. XIII, No. 2, June 1984). It was a taking stock, it helped in clarifying concepts and focused attention on what new directions Indian dance could take.

The connection between art and life, posing radical questions on form, the relevance of the mythological content, religiosity, rigid standardization leaving no room for exploration, quantification, mindlessness, security within tradition, contentment, and other aspects were discussed. Chandralekha raised several questions: Why have classical Indian dances become insular and unresponsive to the dramatic social, historical, scientific, human changes that have occurred in the world during the past thirty years? What makes them resistant to contemporary progressive values? Why have

3
E. Krishna Iyer, lawyer and freedom fighter, played a key role in reviving Bharata Natyam. Photograph courtesy of the late E. Krishna Iyer.

attempts not been encouraged to explore the power and strength of the forms and their links with the martial arts?

The criteria, the parameters, the references, the directions for what constitutes "new" and "contemporary" in the realm of classical dance is a sensitive area and there can be no easy formulae and solutions. The absence of serious and integrated intellectual inputs also has been acutely felt. What kind of scholarship is available to us today compared to those 10th-century stalwarts Abhinavgupta and Nandikeshwara who enunciated radical and loaded concepts for human self-renewal?

Despite the lack of scholarship and theoretical discourse, a dialogue has begun among the practitioners and those who observe the dance scene, which has helped new directions in Indian dance grow in terms of innovative work, experimentation, and contemporary Indian dance to portray contemporary issues.

One sees a definite shift in the thematic content and the search for a new kinetic language is on. Even within the traditional forms like Bharata Natyam, the kinetic language has changed. By building up the linkages with the martial arts like Kalaripayattu and yoga, one notices that the character of the movement of the dance has altered. The innovations within the traditional forms are equally important.

The awareness about the "male gaze", the point of view of women, woman as object of pleasure, the depiction of women in thematic content, and other issues have come in for critical examination. The feminist discourse, the appropriation of art from the devadasi class, the element of sanitization under the

5
Balasaraswati, the legendary
Bharata Natyam dancer from
the devadasi community.
Photograph: Subodh Chandra.

4
Mylapore Gowri Amma, a well
known devadasi, taught
Bharata Natyam to the
legendary Balasaraswati and
also to Rukmini Devi.
Photograph courtesy Sangeet
Natak Akademi, New Delhi.

6–8

Rukmini Devi Arundale, from a brahman family, studied ballet with Anna Pavlova's assistant Cleo Nordi. On the advice of Pavlova, Rukmini Devi turned to Indian classical dance and studied Bharata Natyam under Mylapore Gowri Amma and Meenakshisundaram Pillai. Photographs courtesy (figure 6) Louise Lightfoot collection, Monash University, Melbourne; (figures 7 and 8) courtesy Kalakshetra Foundation, Chennai.

mistaken notion of cleansing the art, the emphasis on the element of bhakti shringara, the origins of dance and the issue of "invented tradition", the re-examination of the fundamental concepts of the *Natyashastra*, the exploration of the energizing principles of dance, and a corrective to the imbalanced approach to dance have been addressed by the dancers. In the case of forms like Bharata Natyam and Kathak though the format of solo dance appears to be threatened at the moment, fresh directions are opening out in the area of group choreographic works, seeking new locations and new identities.

Today Indian dance has to face many challenges and problems. Advanced technology, the proscenium stage, ever increasing and changing audiences, electronic media, globalization, easy access to information, and exposure to various art forms are bound to affect India's dance traditions. Indian dance is poised at a most interesting turn.

New Directions

The present volume on new directions in Indian dance was conceived in 1997 after Marg's revised edition of *Bharata Natyam* was published. The aim was to present 20th-century innovations in Indian dance.

Some of the contributors to this volume attended the East-West Dance Encounter in January 1984 and also the one which followed in 1985, both in Bombay. In 1986 at Rabindra Bharati University, Calcutta, a three-day seminar and a dance festival were organized dealing with innovations in Indian dance. Another major conference took place in Toronto in February 1993, organized by Kalanidhi run by Sudha Khandwani and

Rasesh Thakkar, with financial assistance from the Canadian government. They succeeded in drawing attention to the innovative works of Chandralekha, Kumudini Lakhia, Daksha Sheth, Uttara Asha Coorlawala, to name a few, and also Indian dancers/choreographers based in the UK, USA, and Canada. A similar conference was held in New Delhi in September of the same year, where most of the dancers, scholars, and critics who had participated in the 1984 Bombay event, were invited. Once again the initiative was taken by Georg Lechner, then Director of Max Mueller Bhavan, New Delhi.

These encounters and conferences drew attention to the fact that there are dancers/

9
Madame Menaka, from a Bengal brahman family, was also inspired by Anna Pavlova and studied Kathak from the traditional masters. Photograph courtesy Sunil Kothari dance collection.

10
Poet Vallathol Narayana Menon, founder of Kerala Kala Mandalam, Cheruturuthi, near Shornur. Photograph courtesy Sunil Kothari dance collection.

choreographers working consistently, trying to extend the horizons of Indian dance and seeking new directions. Their works have received an enthusiastic response, creating a climate for innovation. And those who prefer and continue to be creative within the traditional forms, coexist with the new directions. The focus in this volume is on creativity which extends horizons, thematic content, and kinetic language.

Today innovative Indian dance, described variously as Experimental, Contemporary, Modern, has come to be recognized within India as well as internationally. To an extent it has enabled audiences to recognize the existence of Indian Modern Dance. We reprint here Dr Kapila Vatsyayan's seminal article on Uday Shankar, with an Afterthought about the need for a discourse on Modern Dance.

So far writings on the subject have tended to be in the nature of personalized narratives. There has not been a rigorous critical discourse. This is only natural as there has to be a sufficient body of work available for critics to study trends and arrive at theories and standards of criticism. In the two decades since 1984, theory seems to have lagged behind, though dancer/choreographer Uttara Asha Coorlawala's thesis "Classical and Contemporary Indian Dance" (submitted to New York University, 1994) was a major attempt in critical analysis and evaluation of contemporary works. Serious evaluations are made in symposia and dancers explain the raison d'etre of their works to audiences at festivals.

Dancers/choreographers like Mrinalini Sarabhai and Kumudini Lakhia have through

11
A sequence from a Kathakali dance drama at Kerala Kala Mandalam: Ravana with his consort Mandodari.
Photograph: Subodh Chandra.

their writings explained how they have sought new directions in Bharata Natyam and Kathakali, and Kathak, respectively. Chandralekha in her article succinctly touches upon the theoretical issues. The late Manjusri Chaki Sircar and her late daughter Ranjabati have dealt with Rabindranath Tagore's concept of modernization of Indian dance and how through their Navanritya, new dance, they attempted to create a new genre of Indian dance. I have in my article on Manipuri given examples of the shift in thematic content and the evolution of a new kinetic language using martial arts like Thang-ta. Regrettably, in spite of our best efforts, we did not succeed in getting a contribution from the field of Kathakali, though there have been notable experiments with major works like "Othello" and "Faust", to mention just two.

Daksha Sheth narrates various stages of her career and choreographic works and through that we are able to gauge what a radical dancer of the young generation she is. Uttara Asha Coorlawala's analysis of her choreographic work "Winds of Shiva" shows how a dancer dividing her time between two cultures negotiates creative impulses. Astad Deboo, in his fascinating account has described how his tireless struggle has paved the way for another face of Indian dance.

Today it is impossible to ignore the dance sequences of Bollywood films, a genre of their own. Arundhathi Subramaniam observes rightly that dance in Hindi cinema today remains the heterogeneous, irrepressibly parodic composite genre that it always has been. Dynamic, richly diverse, and flagrantly inconsistent, it seems to revel in defying every definition that one seeks to bestow on it.

Indian dance is now part of the international dance scene and Indians abroad have also contributed much to its growth. Sanjoy Roy, analysing the works of Shobana Jeyasingh, Mavin Khoo, and Akram Khan deals with trends in London, whereas Mamata Niyogi-Nakra explains how Bharata Natyam has evolved in America and Canada. Uttara Asha Coorlawala's final article "Re-inscribing Indian Dance" is an exercise in summing up various dilemmas and issues which have arisen with this movement towards new directions.

The uniqueness of this panorama of new directions in Indian dance lies in the "voice" of the creators/dancers and choreographers. To verbalize a non-verbal art demands a certain discipline and the ability to articulate the issues. That these have been communicated here in a lucid manner speaks volumes for the artists' concerns. The accompanying visuals complement their writings, providing a new imagery of Indian classical dance forms.

My thanks to the many friends and colleagues who helped me to bring out this volume.

Note
Most of the articles for this volume were submitted in 2001–02, and reflect trends until that time.

EARLY EXPERIMENTS

modern dance: the contribution of uday shankar and his associates

Kapila Vatsyayan

Many decades ago, when Uday Shankar (1900–77) came into contact with the great Russian ballerina Anna Pavlova (1882–1931), he had as much to give her as to receive from her. On a quite different plane, the visit of Rabindranath Tagore to Southeast Asia resulted in an awareness of the radiance which lay behind a dusty mirror. Only a creative mind like Uday Shankar and a literary genius like Rabindranath Tagore could have, in one stroke, shattered the prejudices against an art which had been relegated to the status of entertainment of a dubious nature.

Rabindranath Tagore received back from Southeast Asia what India had given to that region many centuries ago. In the theatrical field, he received the operatic forms, which had almost been lost to the sophisticated Indian theatre of the 19th century. An experience of Balinese and Javanese dancing made him curious about similar sources in India. His curiosity bore fruit and the first

concrete step was taken when he invited Guru Nabhakumar of Tripura to visit Santiniketan. Far away in Paris, Uday Shankar also found himself looking back to his native land when he realized that the dancers of the West, whether Pavlova or Ruth St Denis or, for that matter, even the German pioneers, were turning towards the "Orient" for fresh inspiration.

The homeward journey for Uday Shankar was an involved one. He began his career as a painter and although he had been brought up to respond to traditional music, he was perhaps not yet ready to dig deep into the vast storehouse of Indian myth and legend and the mysterious recesses of the Indian dance tradition. His experiments were thus of two kinds. The first may be termed as the desire for revival in which Indian mythology and legend were presented through beautiful

spectacle. The second was the expression of the sensitive man's reaction to the ugly mechanization of life. The first few numbers choreographed by Uday Shankar fell into two distinct forms. For the myth and legend he utilized long, flowing, languorous movements in a slow tempo, usually executed to *ektala* or *teentala*. For numbers like "Labour and Machinery", he used jerky movements which were not necessarily based on any *tala* and were not performed to any given raga. Only percussion was used as accompaniment.

Uday Shankar may or may not have done it knowingly, but he had, by adopting these two distinct modes, laid the foundation of what may be termed modern dance as opposed to any of the classical Indian dance forms. His style came to be known as the "Oriental Dance". A parallel development was taking place, which may be called the growth of revivalism. It was the work of the neo-traditionalists, inspired by Rabindranath Tagore, since they were trying to do what Tagore had done in literature, poetry, painting, and the realm of theatre. Looking at the past, they were trying to recreate it as best they could; yet they were trying to present it in as palatable a fashion as possible or at least as they thought people would best receive it. The work of Menaka, Gopinath, Ragini Devi, and even the earlier work of Rukmini Devi may be considered as belonging to this school. Many of these artists, as they went along, discovered deeper roots. Their art was shaped and chiselled in accordance with their discoveries of the tradition, lying mouldy, dusty, but genuine. None of these artists ever attempted to get away from the two cardinal principles of classical Indian dance: the relationship of the music and the *tala* to movement in the abstract dance portions (*nritta*), and the relationship of the word to the movement in the mimetic portions (*abhinaya*). It was not important whether the *nritta* was complex or not, whether the *abhinaya* was traditional or not, and whether it was lengthened over a period of time. The significant fact was their strict adherence to the classical pattern of relating movement to the metrical cycle (*tala*) and to the literary word (*sahitya*).

In contrast, at least in the initial stages of his work, what Uday Shankar did was to break away from this classical pattern. The

distinction between *nritta* and *abhinaya* was broken. It was movement of the human form for its own sake, primary and not dependent on the *tala* or the poetic line. Dance was created first and then music was composed for the dance. This reversed the classical pattern where the musical composition was basic and the dance was adapted to it. In the new formula, movement had to evolve first and it was not guided by any stylized pattern; any point of articulation of the body could be used. Once the number was choreographed, music could be composed for it. Further, except for some singing in order to create an atmosphere, there was hardly any vocal accompaniment in these compositions. It was instrumental music which either heightened the effect of the dance or was subordinate to the movement of the dance. The dancer was no longer in a position to interpret or improvise according to the poetic line or the recurrent musical melody.

Another significant step was also taken. The dance was no longer based on a distinctive kinetic hypothesis; there was no

basic pose which had to be repeated. In the classical pattern, sequential movements emerged from the basic pose, and movement returned to the stillness of the basic sculpturesque pose. In the new dance, there was no self-imposed limitation of either the *ardhamandali* of Bharata Natyam, or the *chauka* of Odissi, or the erect spinal treatment of Kathak, or the figure eight of Manipuri. Movements were chosen for their expressive quality rather than for the abstract pattern which they could evolve on a given geometrical motif. Thus, dancers moved in any direction, had movements at all levels, and these movements were not chunks of time in a variety of rhythmical permutations and combinations like *toda* or *tiramanam* or the *kalasam*. Instead, they were a continuous series of movements against counts or beats. Finally, since there was no poetry to be sung,

there was no need to present variations on a given word or a given line of poetry through gestures, especially of the hands. The story was now told through a series of movements in which the *hastabhinaya* played a very subsidiary role. Indeed it would be more correct to say that the hands did not perform the same function here as they did in any of the classical styles.

Soon, perhaps all too soon, Uday Shankar discovered like his contemporaries that there was the rich storehouse of the classical styles to be explored, and there were those gurus of gigantic stature at whose feet he had to sit to know more. The establishment of the Almora Centre was a welcome step, but it had its own built-in risks. By inviting Guru Kandappa and Guru Namboodripad and Guru Amubi Singh to the Centre, Uday Shankar was exposing his dancers to the experience of classical styles

4
A sequence from the ballet "Labour and Machinery", reflecting the reaction of the sensitive man to the ugly mechanization of life. Photograph courtesy Amala Shankar.

which had emerged through centuries of practice and ruthless crystallization. Understandably and naturally, the majority of the dancers who were pupils of these masters were influenced by one or the other style, which led to modern dance using it as raw material for new creations.

The break-up of the Centre and the establishment of various schools all over the country by artists who had been members of the Centre may be called the second phase of

11. The last battle between Rama and Ravana

5
Shanti Bardhan, Uday Shankar's pupil, choreographed "Ramayana" in which performers acted as puppets.
a. Hanuman crossing the ocean.
b. Jatayu fighting Ravana who has kidnapped Sita.
c. Ravana and Rama in a fight.
Photographs courtesy Rang-Sri Little Ballet Troupe, Bhopal.

6
A sequence from the ballet "Panchatantra" choreographed by Shanti Bardhan in which the movements of the birds and animals were his innovative contribution. Photograph courtesy Rang-Sri Little Ballet Troupe, Bhopal.

the development of modern dance in India. Once away from the creative genius of Uday Shankar and divorced from his tremendous sense of showmanship, the majority of these artists fell back on the known and tested traditional language of the classical styles. By and large, their creations slowly went back to depend upon given musical compositions as on known musical themes. When they ran out of the vocabulary of the dance as imbibed from the gurus, they drew upon the other styles for their expression. Thus, most of the dance-dramas can be analysed in terms of the incipient classical style which lies behind any modern dance creation. These artists returned to a dependence on the language of gesture, foot movement, or rhythmic composition. The only new thing that they did was to have a story in which characters played a part, rather than have one person depicting various roles as in solo dance forms such as Bharata Natyam and Kathak.

It may also be said that none of the followers of Uday Shankar evolved a distinct style which could be termed as his or her individual style, as opposed to Uday Shankar's

own style of movement. It may also be said that none of these artists could really break away from the tested parameters on which classical styles were built. But because the training of these artists in the classical vocabulary was limited, they looked towards a mixture of classical forms. The net result of the composition, more often than not, was a stringing together of various types of movements drawn from the different classical styles. Very often, the frontal vertical movement of Kathak was followed by the triangular terse lines of a Bharata Natyam pattern, and the movement culminated with the vigorous finale of Kathakali. An individual character of movement was lost in the process. Sometimes a slightly greater degree of cohesiveness was achieved because different characters in a dance-drama executed different types of movements based on the different classical styles. This too, however, was not a very satisfactory way of evolving a new movement.

It may be said that the dance-dramas which have been created to date have all been based on one or the other of the classical styles or on a number of classical styles. For example, the dance-dramas of Mrinalini Sarabhai are in Bharata Natyam and Kathakali, those of Triveni Kala Sangam by R.K. Singhjit Singh are in Manipuri, and those of Bharatiya Kala Kendra (now renamed Shriram Bharatiya Kala Kendra) when they introduced Mayurbhanj Chhau for training also used that technique in some of their productions. The dance-dramas of the Indian National Theatre and Sachin Shankar Ballet Unit have followed a variety of classical styles, while the Ramlila of Shriram Bharatiya

Kala Kendra is based on several folk styles with a slight impress of Kathakali. Not one of them can, however, be said to have evolved a style of movement which was personal to the director of the company. In some cases such as the dance-dramas by traditional gurus like Vempati Chinna Satyam who choreographs in Kuchipudi, Guru Kelucharan Mahapatra in Odissi, and Pandit Birju Maharaj in Kathak, we notice that they choreograph the dance-dramas in the technique in which they are comfortable. Some of these have been very serious and successful attempts nonetheless.

A solitary exception among Uday Shankar's pupils was the late Shanti Bardhan. He had imbibed not only the technique of Uday Shankar's style but also the spirit which had inspired Uday Shankar to create a new form of dance. Shanti Bardhan, after breaking away from the Almora Centre, created two ballets which may be correctly termed "modern dance". The first of these was the "Ramlila" in which human dancers acted as puppets. He chose for this ballet one single movement and limited himself to it. Through this limitation, he projected the story of the Ramayana and gave it a unique character. The work was as refreshing as it was new. This approach was a departure from anything that had been done earlier and it was a new vocabulary of modern dance. In his second composition, "Panchatantra", Shanti Bardhan

7
A sequence from "Mukhantar" (Face over Face). Narendra Sharma was another pupil of Uday Shankar, his long career spanning more than fifty years. In this production by his Bhoomika Creative Dance Centre, the dance sequence moves along with images and characters in changing head-gear and masks, allowing the audience to interpret these as they feel. Photograph courtesy Bhoomika Creative Dance Centre, New Delhi.

again created a distinct form; he did not base himself on any classical technique and did not borrow from different sources in order to create a new ballet. He created a distinctly new style. The arm movements, as also the treatment of the spine and the knees, were a real contribution to modern dance. In this ballet, or at least the first half, there was no relationship between word and mime. Nor was there any relationship of a given metrical cycle and footwork. Shanti Bardhan had gone a step further than his master by moving away altogether from the word–gesture relationship, by discarding the statuesque, and by ignoring the *tukda* or *toda* principle. Unfortunately, he did not live to complete his work and his colleagues in the troupe did not have the creative genius required to carry on his tradition. Some of the later creations, even of this troupe, were a retrograde step as they went back to the poetic word and to the elaborate system of *tala*.

In order to complete the picture of those early attempts at creating modern dance, one must mention another important aspect of the modern dance-drama. Creators in this field have not really felt the need to break away from the traditional themes. There has been an attempt to reinterpret the Ramayana, the Mahabharata, and other myths and legends. Whenever they have tried to look for something new and contemporary, the one source which has attracted choreographers has been *The Discovery of India*. This famous book by Jawaharlal Nehru has played an extremely significant role in the history of the modern dance movement. Since 1942, about six versions of this book have been presented. However, when examined closely, it will be found that *The Discovery of India* was only a peg on which to hang the dance-drama. In fact, it was just the presentation of a series of episodes from the history of India chosen at the dancers' or the choreographers' discretion. It had little or nothing to do with the point of view expressed by Nehru or with his intellectual interpretations of the history of India. What had attracted the choreographers was the spectacle and at best the usual moral overtones of stories about the life of Shivaji or the court of Akbar. Till as recently as the mid-1980s and early '90s, practically no one had attempted to present modern themes, except for a few choreographers who were drawn to folk themes. Therefore the idiom has remained for the most part either traditional or neo-traditional because the movements were conditioned by the themes presented. The challenge that dance faces today is new to it. With the throwing open of classical dance forms to vast heterogeneous audiences, changes have taken place and are being made in the tradition itself. The classical styles themselves may get transformed into something new and modern.

Afterthought

Sunil Kothari sought my permission to reprint the article above on Modern Dance written three decades ago. At that time, I had also written two other pieces: an article "Is there a modern dance?" and an editorial on recreating a tradition, in *Sangeet Natak Journal* 49, July–September 1978, dedicated to Uday Shankar. Both these are relevant and complementary to the article now being reprinted.

These articles reflect and articulate the comprehension of developments in what has been termed "Modern Dance" or "Contemporary Dance". Dr Kothari believes that these articles have historical value. I would agree, even if hesitatingly, that perhaps they do have some value in the historiography of the critical evaluation of new trends in Indian dance at the urban level.

During the three decades since then, many momentous developments have taken place: a serious cognizance of these has to be made. While other articles in the volume no doubt voice the authentic experience of the creators

8
In "Conference" choreographed by Narendra Sharma, the element of humour is explored brilliantly. The conference is about the child, but the participants forget the child, arguing aimlessly. Photograph: Bhoomika Creative Dance Centre, New Delhi.

9
In "Flying Cranes" Narendra Sharma employs Chhau in the spreadeagled backward leg throws of the white costumed dancers, the hands held out with the forefinger and thumb in V shape, investing the work with unusual beauty and strength. Photograph: Bhoomika Creative Dance Centre, New Delhi.

KAPILA VATSYAYAN

10
A dramatic moment enacted by Narendra Sharma in "Antim Adhyay" (The Last Chapter). The theme of death has been handled in an imaginative manner. Sharma seeks, with an asceticism and profound understanding of his art, to continue the Uday Shankar legacy today. The result is a free expressive dance theatre which allows the form to emerge from the issues under examination. Photograph: Pradeep Bhatia, courtesy Bhoomika Creative Dance Centre, New Delhi.

of the fresh sensibilities and the multiple flowerings, perhaps there is room to state that, unlike the other arts, no linear graph of developments could be chalked out. There is a concurrency of varied explorations. On the one hand, the neo-classical styles themselves have undergone important transformations, both at the level of essence as also content, form, and technique. There is, on the other hand, a purposive desire to discard some sociological context at the level of content and meaning and yet retain or certainly depend heavily on the chiselled kinetic vocabulary of one or more of the neo-classical styles. Equally significant is the attempt to give new and contemporary reinterpretation to old themes and narrative. Besides, contemporary literature – poetry and prose – has been utilized for dance-compositions, both in the neo-classical styles as also in what is termed modern or contemporary dance. While some continue to be inspired by the vast

corpus of Indian myth and legend and their new interpretation, e.g. ecology, gender issues, dominance and subordination, others have chosen to focus on sociological issues with or without the help of contemporary literature. Very few have identified deeper perennial levels of thought embedded in the Indian tradition which are as old as new.

If at the level of content, meaning, and theme there is the phenomenon of exploring and utilizing the continuing ancient, at the level of form there has been the impressive development of utilizing the movement vocabulary of the vast storehouse of genres and forms roughly called traditional, folk, and tribal – all debatable labels. This exposure to and exploration of these has enriched the contemporary dance vocabulary in many interesting ways. The Chhau forms have been generously utilized, so also the movements of

Kapila Vatsyayan

Kalari and Thang-ta and others, especially from Kerala.

One consequence of this has been that at the level of technique, lower limb and specially leg extensions, elevations, and floor movements are far more in evidence than in the era of Uday Shankar and his contemporaries. Another consequence has been the exploration of geometrical space at floor level and in choreographical patterns. The two, along with other impulses, have amounted to some productions achieving a high level of abstraction comparable to trends in the visual arts. The classification of *nritta* and *abhinaya* is no longer relevant, nor sometimes the sequential storyline.

Besides those who are embedded in the Indian dance forms, there have been others who were exposed to and some trained in one or the other school of Western Modern Dance. Their contemporary Indian dance is of significance. It is clear from the performances of some amongst these few that they have enriched the Indian dance scene in a

distinctive way. Their work is neither imitative of the West nor a refashioning of the tradition by discarding context and retaining technique. Theirs is an individual statement, without being either parochial or global, in a vague sense. In one or two cases their art has captured the predicament of the modern human as he or she faces the future.

These few supplementary remarks were necessary to reiterate that the articles written in the 1970s reflect the situation of that time and day and not of this time and day. Perhaps it has to be added that the proliferation and eclecticism in performance is alas not matched by an equally invigorating and dispassionate critical discourse. Descriptive or personal accounts, or passionate debates on specific positions, are not a substitute for a theoretical framework or non-biased critical analysis. Perhaps and hopefully there will be another generation of not only artists but also others with sharper facilities of analysis and critical appraisal. In the absence of this balance both the theoretical and performative will not achieve the much needed rigour in an important domain of Indian creativity.

Note

This article was first published in *Indian Classical Dance* by Kapila Vatsyayan (first edition, New Delhi, 1974). It is reprinted here with the permission of the Publications Division, Ministry of Information and Broadcasting, Government of India, New Delhi. The writer added the Afterthought specially for this book.

tagore and modernization of dance

Manjusri Chaki Sircar

The dance culture inspired by Rabindranath Tagore (1861–1941) represents not only an era of vibrant creativity, but also a breakthrough in the modernization of the Indian dance scene. It is surprising how in a period of classical dance revivalism, Tagore felt the need for modern tools to express his poetic mind. His prolific output of dance scripts and compositions covers a vast range from narratives to abstract images, demanding a wide selection of dance vocabulary. To appreciate Tagore's vision of dance we must remember that although he wrote in his vernacular Bengali, his creative efflorescence can be appreciated and shared by people all over the world. His vision of dance as well as his paintings, music, and above all, his writings cannot be understood in the context of a parochial culture. In Santiniketan, he encouraged young dancers to draw material from different classical sources and folk traditions. He kept his doors open to ideas from both the Eastern and the Western worlds. In this way, his concept of dance became enriched, while still remaining deeply rooted in Indian culture. Unfortunately, after his death in 1941, the creativity and growth of this dance style stagnated. For some conservative "Tagoreans" it is taboo even to imagine that further evolution or development of this creative dance language is possible.

It is interesting to examine the early motivation behind Tagore's search for a new dance vocabulary and its growth and development. His eagerness to develop a contemporary style of dance is evident from his restless search for a dance language from different parts of India, even across national boundaries. Between 1919 and 1924 Tagore travelled frequently all over India and abroad. His deep interest in dance is expressed in his letters from Japan. He writes: "...this dance seems to be the song of movements. There is not even a trace of low physicality in the gesture of the body." This comment is significant in the context of the decadent "nautch" culture prevailing in Calcutta in the early 20th century.

At Santiniketan, under his guidance, dancers absorbed movements from Kandyan, Javanese, and European folk dances. The poet was fascinated by the freedom of movement in European modern and impressionist dance, while the delicate structure of the Javanese dance-drama inspired him to create an original form of dance-drama. Protima Devi, an artist herself and the daughter-in-law of Tagore, was impressed during their tour of England in 1930 by ballet choreography rehearsals at Dartington Hall. On her return she introduced large group dances with varied movements and rhythm presented in unison with spatial patterns formed by the dancers. The costumes of the dancers designed by great artists like Nandalal Bose and Protima Devi were influenced by Javanese dance costumes, Ajanta frescos, and folk motifs, but were integrated into an original style typical of early Santiniketan performances.

Tagore's contribution to the modernization of Indian dance cannot be compared with the revival of ancient dance forms which was taking place elsewhere in the country. He was inspired by tradition to move forward to an artistic future where form and content would match each other through an innovative process. To Tagore dance was the natural human instinct of spontaneous physical expression of varied emotions. In the last years of his life there was a youthful drive in him to visualize an interpretation of his music and poetry through dance. Interestingly, this is also the period when his imagination expressed itself through modern abstract impressionist paintings.

This period of Tagore's life is a very important one in the cultural history of India. A creative era often finds its expression in the milieu of social progress. This was the era of rapid change generated by an awakening of national pride and a questioning of traditional mores like caste discrimination, social hierarchy, and polarity of sex roles. Contemporary literature reflects a drastic change in the attitude towards the male–female relationship and in the expected role models. The thematic content of Tagore's dance lyrics was undeniably a reflection of his time and often much ahead of it. The mode of presentation, with equal participation of the male and the female on stage, created a visual confirmation of the new era in Indian society. Tagore's charismatic presence in a corner of

1
Jorasanko, Gurudev Rabindranath Tagore's residence at Kolkata. Photograph: Ashok Ghosh.

the stage as *sutradhara* and the dignity and refinement of the performance brought it ready acceptance among audiences in different parts of India, Ceylon (Sri Lanka), and wherever the company toured.

In Tagore's lifetime Santiniketan became a centre imbued with the aesthetics of literature, arts, crafts, music, and dance. Artists and scholars from different parts of India and abroad collaborated with the founding father. The poet believed that dance had an important place in a healthy social environment and was meaningful for today's existence. A collective team of highly gifted musicians, singers, artists, and others worked with a group of young dancers. Artists like Nandalal Bose and Protima Devi created sophisticated stage sets, props, make-up, costumes, light design, and overall colour schemes. The effect was remarkably original.

The rich musical structure of Tagore's compositions and the depth and subtlety of the imagery of his poetry needed expression in dynamic movements in a style far removed from the classical. The vital period of development of this style can be placed between 1921 and 1940, of which the last years were the most vibrant. In the beginning, dance movements were just embellishments to the songs. Simple and spontaneous movements, mostly from preliminary Manipuri and available folk styles were used. Gradually the poet gave more emphasis to dance training. He encouraged his young dancers, all trainees, to learn more and improve their technique. In later years Kathakali and Manipuri were taught by gurus from Kerala Kala Mandalam and Manipur. During Tagore's lifetime, the list of teachers at Sangeet

Bhavan, who worked from three months to three years or more at a stretch, included three in Kathakali, eight in Manipuri, one in Mohini Attam, and one in Javanese style. Along with these styles, Garba from Gujarat, Bengal's Baul, and Hungarian and Russian folk dances were also absorbed.

In 1931, Protima Tagore returned from Europe after three years of training in European modern dance under the guidance of Rudolf Laban, Kurt Joss, and Mary Wigman. On her return she choreographed Tagore's poem "Jhulan", recited by the poet himself. Reflecting on this Tagore writes:

> She takes delight in evolving new dance forms of her own rhythmic representation of ideas…. She is alert and vigorous and the cadence of her limbs carries the expression of an inner meaning and never an exhibition of skill bound by some external canons of tradition.

This comment encapsulates Tagore's essential concept of dance.

However, such encouragement of exposure to non-Indian styles should not be misunderstood as Tagore's way of modernization. His psyche was deeply embedded in Indian aesthetics. The idea of borrowing was not eclecticism, but rather absorption and assimilation into a "chemical synthesis". The poet constantly sought more exposure to other dance forms. He sent Santidev Ghosh to Kerala in 1931 and to Bali in 1939. At one time he was very eager to appoint a teacher of Mayurbhanj Chhau, which, however, did not materialize. In his own words: "It would take years to learn their dance properly. But it would not be difficult to collect some basic dance movements. We do not need more than that. It would be detrimental to suppress our own dance under imitation of theirs." The poet disliked the endless repetition of classical styles and sometimes complained about such tiresome sights as taught by gurus.

Recently there have been assertions in some quarters that any dance based on narratives is passe. The concept of creative arts without narratives has been popular in the West since the 1920s, especially in the case of painting ("modernism") and literature.

It would be immature and misleading to give up the entire *nritya* tradition in favour of only pure dance movements, a step that may further encourage "cultural colonialism" by the West. Even as they keep their eyes open to the outside world, Indian dancers have to find their own path toward modernization – a process which, however, should be rooted in our soil. It should be noted that, despite a distinct and rich tradition, modern dance in Eastern countries like China, Japan, and the Philippines, has moved towards the Western mode. A presentation by my troupe evoked an interesting comment from the South Asian audience: "Whenever we think Modernization, we associate it with Westernization. But your process appears so different – something that has grown out of your own culture."

It is true that the traditional narrative culture in India represents a patriarchal ethos ensuring an inferior role for women, which is demeaning for both women and men. A change in this unequal status is urgently called for and the Indian dancer of today

bears a heavy moral responsibility in this respect. Re-creation of old narratives, therefore, needs to be done which would then require a different mode of presentation. The psycho-emotional content of the *nritya* tradition can open up new vistas which could break down the narrative/non-narrative dichotomy. The transformation of traditional narratives through a metamorphic process can have immense possibility for Indian dancers. Discarding the narratives completely would alienate dance from the larger audiences and confine it to a limited number of intellectuals seeking purely cerebral pleasure.

Modernization of dance need not be a replacement of tradition, but can be an evolutionary change in the latter. This evolution is particularly significant in Tagore's narratives, which are the creation of a very modern mind. All of his narratives and lyrics are free from the conventional religiosity; they are inspired by what can be termed "spiritual humanism". Tagore's women are not moulded in the model of classical *nayika*s. There is also no attempt to glorify femininity with the religious aura of Shakti, the feminine energy. Such glorification often blurs the issue of women's basic human rights. Tagore's women are self-respecting, self-reliant, and sensuous human beings. A modern dancer has to find an innovative vocabulary to depict such women. There is also the immense possibility of abstract or impressionist interpretation of his poems and lyrics.

The thematic content of Tagore's dance-dramas, songs, and poetry called for innovation in the technique of dancing. His themes reflected the ethos of the modern age. Below are some examples of his narrative-based dance-dramas which demand a modern approach in choreography.

Chandalika

This is a reinterpretation of a Jataka story. In Tagore's storyline, the women have a vibrant sexuality of an autochthonous culture, not under the oppressive brahmanic tradition. Prakriti, the heroine, rebels against the practice of caste discrimination. In the prose-play she addresses the Buddhist monk Ananda: "I have brought you down to the dust.... Otherwise, how would you rescue me from it?"

Chitrangada

This dance-drama is a fresh interpretation of the Mahabharata legend with a redefinition of the male–female relationship. Towards the end of this romantic dance-drama the warrior princess affirms: "I am Chitrangada, the princess and not a devi, nor an ordinary woman. I am not the one to be placed above and worshipped; nor to be left behind as a subordinate. Only when you let me be by your side in prosperity and adversity will you then know me."

Tasher Desh

Here the poet presents a stagnant society bound by rigid canons and scriptures. Undoubtedly, this is a satire on the traditional moribund Indian society. The poet dedicated the work to the fiery young revolutionary Subhas Chandra Bose. In the story, a restless prince and his companion find themselves shipwrecked in the "Land of Cards". The inhabitants wear the restrictive garb of cards and live a rather peaceful and contented,

though drab life. The prince and the companion confront them and gradually their youthful, joyous, and adventurous presence helps the inhabitants to discard the shackles of the age-old society. The prince brings the message of freedom and ultimately wins over the card-humans one by one. In the grand finale, the cards take off their cardboard costumes and dance: "Break the barriers of the dam.... Let the dry bed of the river be flooded with the joyous laughter of life." This call for youthful vigour should be understood in the context of the political milieu of Tagore's time.

Can the progressive ideas of Tagore on modern choreography that are now six decades old, offer inspiration to dancers today? Those of us who search for the greatest degree of contemporaneity in Tagore's work

2
Chandalika, a dance-drama by Gurudev Rabindranath Tagore. The dancers are (left) Nandita Kripalani and Mrinalini Sarabhai. Photograph courtesy Viswabharati Archive, Santiniketan.

look upon the early period as a stepping stone, a point of departure from where to move forward. Another source of inspiration is Tagore's paintings, where there is no trace of familiar poses of classical dance. They are impressionist and emotive of free body lines.

A modern dancer has no scope to be "Rabindrik" in the sense that a singer of Rabindra Sangeet could be. Rabindra Sangeet was developed with a definite system of notation and mode of presentation during Tagore's lifetime (he himself was a gifted musician and highly trained singer). Even then the *gayaki* of Rabindra Sangeet has changed considerably over the past six decades.

As a dancer of today, I am happy to draw my inspiration from Tagore's concept of dance. But when I create dancing, it becomes my own personal artistic expression. It is possible to retain this individuality without being indifferent to Tagore's aesthetics of dance.

When I am inspired by a piece of music or one of his lyrics, I do not simply translate the words into the language of dance. Instead, they become the source of inspiration that helps me to reach out for the dynamics of movement which creates a dance language transcending the words. It is sheer injustice to dance as an art form, if it has to play a subordinate role to music, be it that of Tchaikovsky, Tagore, or Thyagaraja.

The emotive quality of the words and the basic mood of the literature needs to be expressed through a total body language, instead of relying only on *hastamudra*s and *sattvikabhinaya*. In dance I emphasize *anubhava* – the inner feeling of each movement, *komala* (gentle) or *kathora* (hard).

In classical training, the emotional content of the movement is taught much later, after the teaching of the mechanical execution of the pure technique. The dancer is subjected to an extreme separation between abstract movement and felt movement. A fortunate pupil may be encouraged to enjoy a movement with a pleasing smile on the face. The rule, *yato hastah tato drishti* (where the hand goes there go your eyes) denotes an immersed feeling in movement with total concentration. Perhaps this is a way to generate emotion in dance from the beginning of training. However, at present this rule is rarely taught in a classroom situation. The emotional content of the body language in its entirety helps the dancer to cope with varied performance environments, from the proscenium theatre to open-air for a large audience.

The socio-psychological milieu of India has drastically changed over the last sixty years. Tagore's untiring efforts were successful in bringing about an awareness and acceptance of dance as a legitimate social/cultural activity. In the beginning, Manipuri Lasya became the most acceptable form of dance perhaps because of its non-threatening gentleness. The social environment of the poet's time was still very restrictive because of post-Victorian Brahmo puritanism. Contemporary photographs of sari-clad women dancers in costume betray the physical inhibition in their postures. The dancer's body is subjected to various social and cultural pressures. At present, we expect not only far better dancers but also much less inhibited female bodies radiating more confidence and self-assurance. Even the use of salwar-kameez during dance practice helps the dancer to

3–5
Three sequences from "Tomari Matir Kanya",
choreographed by Manjusri Chaki Sircar, based
on the dance-drama and play *Chandalika* by
Tagore. Manjusri explores the rituals of Maya.
In figure 3 the mother and her *bhairavi*s take on
images of rites of passage, with Prakriti as
initiate, being reborn as a woman with mature
sexuality.
In figure 4 the rite of passage is choreographed
imaginatively with Prakriti coming out of a
tunnel formed by the *bhairavi*s.
In figure 5 helpless Prakriti clings to her mother.
Photographs: Avinash Pasricha.

experience greater freedom than a regular sari. Taking these factors into account, we must create dance with the newly-found freedom and the available resources.

By freeing myself from the limitations of one particular style, I can experience the gentle wavy spatial lines of Manipuri as well as the firm controlled and balanced "mandala" in Bharata Natyam, a free run from a spontaneous spirit (here the original source of footwork comes from Kathak's *gat bhava* and from Yakshagana walks), leaps, *utplavana*, or *akashachari bhramari*, a fall, landing in the flying Gandharva posture found in Ajanta frescos and temple sculptures.

An analysis of the *sthanaka*s (body positions) and *hasta*s (hand positions) can help the dancer recognize and execute different modes of tension and balance of muscles and body weight. While Manipuri and Mayurbhanj Chhau help fluid lines and airy elevation respectively, Odissi, Kathakali, and Bharata Natyam provide a strongly grounded quality to the movements. Each one of the above, for its appropriate use, needs to be understood in relation to the source of energy behind the movement.

Such assimilation is possible only with proper training of the dancer and appreciation of the artistic logic of the principles of different classical dances of India. This assimilation is not really a reconstruction, but a growth of dance expression. There is still some reluctance in certain quarters of the dance world to look upon dance movements without the contextual references. Once this cognitive block is removed, it is possible to accept movements from several sources without hesitation.

Over the years we have gradually developed a style of dance which we have termed Navanritya. The style has grown through an evolutionary process which is still continuing. I find it essential to use a codified technique of dance, which makes for its easier transmission to the trainee-dancers who have come from varied backgrounds of classical training, mostly Bharata Natyam, Odissi, and Manipuri. The training helps them to understand the logic and principles of each style of dance. Only then we move forward to innovate new movements from the classical foundation. Sometimes movements from martial arts, like Kalaripayattu, Thang-ta or Mayurbhanj Chhau and even the postures of yogasana, images of sculptures and frescos can inspire dancers to explore the dynamics of expression.

The modernization of dance language had emphatically drawn its strength from the classical resource. Just as in modern Bengali poetry we find the free use of pure Sanskrit words integrated into its inherent structure, so also in modern dance the classical idiom may fit in if used spontaneously. Such an approach opens up immense possibilities for the use of the vast repertoire of classical movements to enrich our modern dance.

I shall now give some examples of how we have used Navanritya in our dance compositions based on the three Tagore compositions mentioned earlier.

Tomari Matir Kanya (1982)

"Tomari Matir Kanya" (Daughter of the Earth) based on Rabindranath Tagore's dance-drama

6
Sequence from "Yugasandhi",
the beginning of a new era.
Manjusri conceived it at a time
when the country was rocked
by communal riots following
the Babri Masjid demolition.
The choreographer's personal
memories of strife-torn India
find expression in this creative
statement against social
violence and disintegration.
The birth of a baby, its tender
touch, adds an incredible
positive twist. Photograph:
Avinash Pasricha.

bhikshu causes natural catastrophe: clouds gather, the sea comes to untimely tide, the sky explodes with thunder, and the monk finally succumbs. But when he arrives, Prakriti realizes that her love for him is only a symbol of the freedom she has achieved through him.

I have tried to place Prakriti in the historical context where her passion, rebellion, and self-realization are the basis of a collective protest and movement against caste dogma. Ananda is not directly shown, for it is the force of his message that works upon Prakriti, becoming physical passion of an isolated moment only in her psyche. The rituals of Maya, the mother, and her *bhairavi*s take on images of rites of passage, with Prakriti as initiate, being "re-born" as a woman with mature sexuality – something that was never taboo in non-brahmanic society. The emphasis in this production is on three aspects: the power of women in religious spheres outside Hindu-brahmanic domain; the self-reliance and self-respect of the untouchable woman; and the force of the oppressed in revolt.

The song "Hridaye mandrilo damaru" indicates the anticipation of a storm in Prakriti's life. To heighten the intensity of Prakriti's emotion I did not go in for literal interpretation, but used a chorus, clad in shades of blue, dancing on a high rostrum, conveying tumultuous desire, while Prakriti expresses her overwhelming passion through floor movements *bhumisparsha* style, in total body language.

In choreographing two "Maya Nrityas", I used impressions of Lai Haraoba, the non-Vaishnavite Manipuri ritual floor designs.

and play, *Chandalika*, derived from the Buddhist Jataka, is about an untouchable girl, Prakriti, who after repeated insults from high-caste girls, first in their play with flowers and then in the company of a curd-seller, falls in love with the Buddhist monk Ananda, who asks her for water and tells her that all humanity is equal, so her touch cannot be impure. She convinces her mother to use the magical power of tantric rituals to draw the monk into her web of desire. The struggle between the earthy power of the mother and the spiritual strength of the

Chitrangada (1988)

The two personalities of "Chitrangada" are usually performed by two different dancers. Originally, the idea was to have one person doing both roles, a challenging task for a dancer. The transformation of warrior Chitrangada, from *kurupa* (unattractive) to *surupa* (beautiful) can be shown only as an external change.

Chitrangada, an independent woman, falls prey to her love for Arjuna, who in turn rejects her because of her unfeminine presence. With the help of Madan, god of love, her desire finds a refuge in the form of a beautiful woman. She wins over Arjuna but proud Chitrangada who allowed herself to be reduced to a mere beautiful woman, felt demeaned by Arjuna's lustful behaviour. In the end, both reach the point of self-realization and are united in love and respect. *Surupa* then changes into *kurupa*, revealing her identity to Arjuna.

"Chitrangada" offers scope for the use of a vast array of dance vocabulary, ranging from the powerful hunting scene to romantic duets. The dance of Madan, celestial god, can be made effective by the use of Mayurbhanj Chhau, whereas the martial arts movements of Thang-ta and Kalaripayattu can be employed for depicting the hunting scene. Such integration of styles should never appear as patchwork; instead the process should create fresh movements out of the old.

Tasher Desh (1990)

"Tasher Desh" (Land of Cards) was originally written as a *natika* with the minimal use of movements with dialogue. When our group was commissioned to present it as a dance-drama, it was necessary to edit the dialogue. The third chapter was reduced to a ten-minute

7
In "Charaiboti", meaning one who moves and continues to search, Manjusri has used movements from her Navanritya with dancers moving in sitting position, creating various levels. The group compositions were highly imaginative. Photograph: Avinash Pasricha.

dance sequence depicting social tension and the pettiness of a closed society. Some key dialogues are retained with musical effects for independent dance expression. The subtle nuances of sarcasm and satire had to be conveyed through movements and gestures.

Traditionally, the cards hardly have any movement. The simplistic movements were changed to more complex and rigid ones reflecting the age-old bondage of social norms. In the popular drama, the queen does not have a strong personality. In our presentation, she is the catalyst to instil the rebellious move among the cards.

In Tagore's time, male roles were frequently performed by women. Though this is no longer the case, in our production the role of the Rajaputra, the prince, is performed by a woman as a double challenge.

In "Tasher Desh" we have used large group dances as "chorus" to represent social turmoil and storm, employing unconventional movements. These are created out of yogasana postures.

Dealing with the narratives of Tagore's dance-dramas we have frequently used chorus, a symbolic device to convey simultaneous multiple interpretations of the theme. For example, the scene of the human tunnel in "Tomari Matir Kanya" takes the audience to an artistic domain far beyond the traditional narrative. It is the expression of the psycho-emotional transformation of a woman. Instead of relying on *sattvikabhinaya*, I designed the scene to show how the childhood stage is transformed into womanhood. In "Maya Nritya", the daughter clinging to her mother like a baby symbolically expresses the helplessness of Prakriti.

In West Bengal I have found that some people, nurtured on (so-called) Tagorean dance, feel uncomfortable without direct transliteration of lyrics into movement, especially in the interpretation of poems and seasonal songs. I stress repeatedly that contemporary dance language is its own entity. The text is only an aural support but any of the dance-pieces could exist independently of text as well. Thus, the relationship between the dance language, the text, and the music, combined with the costumes and other visuals, creates a layering of experiences for the viewer that are interrelated but not entirely interdependent. Over the last ten years, however, the situation has changed.

The ideas of Tagore form a strong basis from which to approach contemporary dance. In terms of a textual and intellectual framework they affirm an aesthetic that is very modern and very Indian. Similarly, the classical and other physical techniques offer a firm base for movement exploration. In my understanding, these bases are a takeoff point for the contemporary sensibility of a choreographer.

Editor's Note

Before Manjusri Chaki Sircar passed away in 2000, she had discussed this article with me, and given me an edited version. The original was published in *Rasa* Volume I, 1995, which I edited.

traditional dance and contemporary choreography

Mrinalini Sarabhai

As a dancer studying the classical dance forms from the traditional gurus in the early 1930s, it was natural for my generation to look at art as an expressive visualization of the spiritual. Learning classical dance during the revival period, we were fired with the spirit of nationalism, seeking our own identity through our indigenous arts, be it music, dance, or painting. From earliest times, the sacred precincts of our temples were the structures within which the magnificent sculptures, the colourful paintings, and the arts of dance, drama, and music were nurtured and dedicated to the Supreme, the eternal source of energy of the Universe.

They were all depictions of a higher sphere, the dance of Nataraja and Parvati in the cosmos aspects of creation, maintenance and dissolution; wisdom and discrimination in the form of Ganapati; Sarasvati, the goddess of learning; Durga upholding dharma; Lakshmi, the goddess of prosperity. It was an exploration of a spiritual dimension to be worshipped, emulated, and brought to earth.

The dance of Nataraja, so wonderfully depicted in the images of the South, caught our imagination for its philosophical concept of the rhythm and unity of life. It is the dancing universe, the ceaseless flow of energy, going through an infinite variety of patterns, melting into one another. For a scientist it is the dance of sub-atomic matter like photographs of a shower of cosmic rays hitting the bubble chamber of interacting particles, which bear testimony to the continual rhythm of the universe. Dr Ananda Coomaraswamy called it "poetry but nonetheless science".

The form of Shiva as Nataraja depicts movement in dance, the continuous cycle of creation, evolution, and destruction. In the backdrop of space, the cosmic dancer performs, creating, destroying, and reaffirming life energy, inspired by the Goddess Shakti, the Absolute (eka) divided into two, the Ardhanarishvara, matter and energy.

Studying Bharata Natyam under the great gurus like Meenakshisundaram Pillai,

Muthukumaran Pillai, Ellappa, and Kitappa, and Kathakali under Guru Kunju Kurup and others, I began to grasp what the dynamism of our dance techniques means. It springs from the concept of timelessness. Bharata's *Natyashastra* clarified the meaning of what role the body plays in dance, as also the flavour of emotional expression. When imbued with the quality of universality, the *rasa*s, says Bharata, arise from the *bhava*s. Commentator Bhatta Nayaka propounding his Theory of Universalization (*sadharanikarana*) emphasized that each *rasa* loses its personal association and a sublimation of the emotion takes place.

I was also overwhelmed by the richness of India's tradition with its myriad deities, the underlying philosophy of the stories and the legends, the meaningfulness of shapes and forms, that create a background that nourishes and inspires. For it is the perennial wisdom of humanity, a yoga that is action binding movement with aspiration.

In the *Mandukya Upanishad* we come across the statement: "Taking as a bow the great weapon of the Upanishad, place upon it an arrow sharpened by meditation, stretching it with a thought, directed to the essence of THAT, penetrate the imperishable as the mark." What imagery! India's philosophy creates wondrous patterns of movements and from that vastness I have often drawn my inspiration. By training under the great masters I acquired the techniques which helped to create the movement. The body then could reproduce the vitality of the forms. The knowledge of the techniques of Bharata Natyam and Kathakali offered scope for the creation of movements. The experience of movement, revealing meaning through the face and the hands, significance in every gesture – be it the lifting of an eyebrow, the widening of the eyes, a slight turn of the head, and the strong language of the body were all available for creating contemporary choreographic works.

1

In her first major work "Manushya" way back in 1949, Mrinalini Sarabhai projected the powerful technique of Kathakali dispensing with traditional Kathakali costumes and make-up, allowing the body to speak. It told the story of humanity in simple terms, from birth to death. Chathunni Panicker played the role of Manushya.

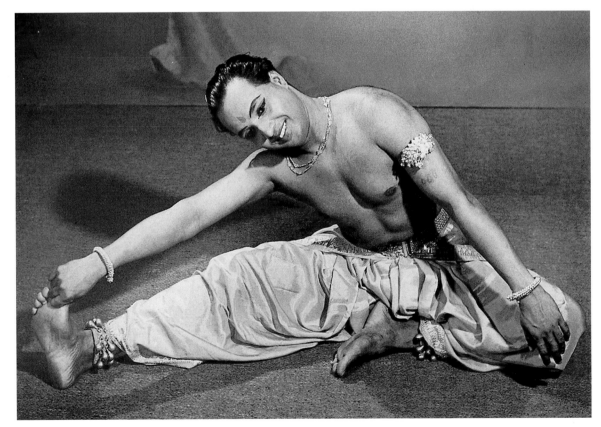

Kathakali enhanced my knowledge of form and expression in the force and powerful movements of our classical arts. Every encounter, involving years of practice, opened up new vistas and I felt as though on a mountain peak having struggled up, now ready to strive for new landscapes of my own discipline, my own language. Several accretions and experiences while growing up, enriched my art. Looking back to my childhood, I realize that perhaps intuitively I must have imbibed the ideas of freedom. There was Gandhiji's satyagraha of non-violence, my mother Ammu Swaminathan's fight for women's rights, the discarding of all foreign elements. The intense patriotism and dedication of those years left an indelible impression on me. And these aspects, as it were, came through in my dance spontaneously. I also realized that to express myself through dance, I would have to experiment and innovate.

My first major work "Manushya" (1949) was designed to project the powerful technique of Kathakali. It told the story of humanity in simple terms, from birth to death. It created a stir and more importantly a debate. I dispensed with the traditional Kathakali costumes and make-up, which are integral to this dance-drama. I let the body speak with Kathakali movements. It was a major breakthrough in terms of taking up a simple theme, not depending upon a mythological story as generally seen in Kathakali. Also with this radical step of the men wearing the normal dhoti, and not the Kathakali costumes, the character became immediately recognizable, with whom one could identify. I attempted that way back in

1949, realizing the need for themes with contemporary sensibilities. It was not easy, for our traditional dance forms are extremely powerful and any innovation poses a tremendous challenge.

Reading, writing, prose and poetry, contributed to my inspiration more than any other art form. Creativity often began with personal experiences. Hearing of women being burnt alive for dowry in Saurashtra disturbed me no end. The piece "Memory" choreographed in Bharata Natyam was charged with dynamism and spoke of social atrocities against women. I explored *sollukattu*s, the mnemonic syllables, as a language. The body language reflected injustice, stress, and atrocities. I attempted to portray the agony of women with which the audiences could identify and find a reflection of themselves. Performed at a time when atrocities against women were not made public, it created a questioning everywhere and also a debate in the print media. The significance had to come from within, in order that the perception translate into a dynamic dance image. Dance could thus be a meaningful vehicle for social change.

After my schooling, I went to the poet Gurudev Rabindranath Tagore's Santiniketan in the late '30s. It was a rare privilege to be with him, sit at his feet, listen to him, sing his songs, and also dance in his dance-dramas and to his poems. His close association has indeed influenced me the most in my artistic endeavours. Gurudev gave me the freedom to express myself in dance. I was lucky to perform lead roles, whether masculine or feminine, in his dance-dramas. I was also asked to choreograph them following my own imagination. This was a liberating process and released me from the bond of specific techniques of dance with which I was familiar. Though these experiments were at Santiniketan in the context of Gurudev's poetry, they stood by me later on when I charted my own path to choreograph issues like untouchability, which Gurudev had touched upon in his dance-drama *Chandalika*. Many years later I choreographed *Chandalika* and brought in the issue of human dignity and equality, depicting the atrocities inflicted upon untouchables and other human beings, which found timely resonances.

I was born into a matrilineal family. Caring deeply about the environment and the hazards of today's civilization was part of my upbringing. I relished Kalidasa's play *Shakuntala* with its beautiful descriptions of nature, and was moved by the injustice meted out to Shakuntala for no fault of hers. I interpreted the play differently and titled it "Curse of Durvasa". The injustice to the young and innocent Shakuntala, the arrogance of the king, and the curse of Durvasa found a different treatment and interpretation. In my concept, all the players epitomized the world and Durvasa, the rishi, represented Destiny moving through each episode. At the end Shakuntala asks each one why they did not tell her about the ring and to Dushyanta, the king, she cries: "If the signet ring of the king is not on my finger, then surely it should be on yours? Would you remember where it was?" She reinforces her sense of self-respect by finally declaring: "I came to the world alone, and I will go out alone."

I am not averse to dancing to mythological themes or stories from the Puranas in order to innovate. It depends upon an interpretation that has contemporary relevance. In the case of Shakuntala it concerns women and their fate and by choreographing a theme from a mythological story I attempt to create an awareness about the plight of women. For this play I use soliloquy as a device, and have employed both Bharata Natyam and Kathakali techniques.

During the early 1970s I planned a work, "Rigveda", which could be danced to silence. Taking the Sanskrit quote *isa vasyam idam sarvam* (all this is for habitation by the Lord) and relating it to *tat tvam asi* (that thou art), suggesting the unity of all existence, an

4
Mallika as Prakriti and Mrinalini as Maya, the mother, in Tagore's *Chandalika*. With a radio commentary in the background on the atrocities against untouchables, performed to the text of the poet, this piece echoes the present-day plight of the oppressed.

5
"Rigveda" was based on an abstract concept. Using Kathakali technique, though dispensing with its colourful costumes and make-up, Mrinalini choreographed a piece danced to silence.

abstract concept, using Kathakali technique, but dispensing with the colourful traditional costumes and make-up, I choreographed a piece of silence. Such explorations extend the frontiers of dance. There is less dependence on *sahitya*. Also, eliminating music creates further responsibility towards integrating the movements artistically.

The issue of pollution is connected with environment. The myth of Ganga being received in the *jata*, locks of Shiva, flowing and giving life to the hundred children of the king, is an interesting one. What has happened to the river Ganga today? Her waters are polluted. Can one depict this in dance to bring the message home? Through the dance movements narrating the story of mythological Ganga the choreography moves to the present, and through words poses the problem. I have attempted to connect mythological events to present-day issues bringing a shift in theme to relate it to contemporary problems.

These choreographic works are related to happenings around the world. Creating a piece

of artistic expression in our contemporary age demands a technique of communication that says something. The content needs expression through a technique which does not use dance forms which are dated, but seeks extension of a kinetic language of the present day and time. And even when a known, familiar technique like Kathakali or Bharata Natyam is used, it appears new and contemporary. It should have that vitality.

We are surrounded today by great technologies, and violence increases day by day. My latest work "This Mahabharata" is drawn from the devastation of the Mahabharata. The words of Bhishma, as he lies dying on the bed of sharp arrows, resounded in my mind: "Because men will not leave their wickedness, because they will not learn to love instead of hate, to give and share instead of to grasp and grab, there has come about the mighty holocaust in which there is indeed neither victor nor vanquished but only death and destruction."

Choreographing themes with contemporary relevance has helped me to understand how one can look at the tradition one has inherited from the past, and use it artistically to make it meaningful. I do not see the traditional forms and the innovative forms as in opposition. But I do believe that the relevance of themes should not be lost sight of and the forms must develop further and not remain ossified.

Photo Credits
All photographs courtesy Darpana Academy of Performing Arts, Ahmedabad.

reflections
on new directions
in indian dance

Chandralekha

One of the crucial experiences that shaped my response and attitude to dance was during my very first public dance recital (*arangetram*) in 1952. It was a charity programme in aid of the Rayalseema Drought Relief Fund. I was dancing "Mathura Nagarilo", depicting the river Yamuna, the water-play of *sakhi*s, the sensuality, the luxuriance, and abundance of water. Suddenly, I froze, with the realization that I was portraying all this profusion of water in the context of a drought. I remembered photographs in the newspapers of cracked earth, of long, winding queues of people waiting for water with little tins in hand. Here, Guru Ellappa was singing "Mathura Nagarilo". Art and life seemed to be in conflict. The paradox was stunning. For that split second I was divided, fragmented into two people.

Through the years this experience has lived with me and I have not been able to resolve the contradiction which, of course, is a social one. On the one hand, a great love for all that is rich and nourishing in our culture and, on the other, the need to contribute positive energies towards changing the harsh realities of life. For me, to be able to respond to the realities of life is as crucial as to remain alive and tuned to sensuality and cultural wealth. I have struggled to harmonize, to integrate these diverging directions in order to remain sensitive and whole.

Being inheritors of colonial structures and institutions of education, language, liberal values, and maybe even notions of aesthetics, we cannot overlook the mediation of the West in shaping our approach to our traditional arts. Problems of revivalism, nostalgia, purity, exclusiveness, conservation, preservation, need to be examined. There is a tendency to swing between the polarities of rejecting the West to seek the security of our little islands, or of accepting the West at the cost of a wealth of traditions and without any attempt to try and listen to what they have to tell us.

Such conflict stems from a lack of consciousness and an inability to comprehend the central and basic issues which, ultimately, are connected with integrated and humanized

1 (*opposite*)
A sequence from "Lilavati", choreographed by Chandralekha.
Using classical Bharata Natyam form "Lilavati" is an interpretation through dance, music, and poetry, of the celebrated text on Indian mathematics by Bhaskaracharya. The text belongs to the period following *Natyashastra* and suggests the organic connection between *natya, kavya, ganita*. A departure in thematic content, it deals with the understanding of unrelated and abstract numbers. Photograph: Sadanand Menon.

existence on our planet. The East in order to be "contemporary" would mean to understand and express the East in its own terms; to explore to the full the linkages generated by valid interdisciplinary principles common to all arts and central to the creative concept of *rasa*; to extend the frontiers of the loaded cultural language of our soil.

I see dance as a visual, tactile, and sensual language, structured with a specific vocabulary and idiom, with a space/time, with organic bind, principles, and most importantly, related to the dynamics of energy and flow with a capacity to recharge human beings. The internal relation between the dance and the dancer and the external relation between dance and society are questions that cannot be taken lightly.

First of all, dance is an expression of physicality. In the course of human evolution, for a long time, physicality was a communal possession to be collectively expressed. The remnants of tribal societies show the basic unity of material life and physical expression. So we start from the fundamental premise that dance does not originate from the heaven, that it has a material base, that it is rooted in the soil, the region, the community, in usages, work rhythms, habits and behaviour, food patterns, and social relations and in racial characteristics like nose, skin, eyes, hair – a whole lot of accumulations that go by the name of culture, and intimately related to body attitudes, physiognomy, and to work and tools. Even in its most stylized form, dance retains a certain universality of idiom and is

an extension of and a supplement to spoken language.

The history of dance, then, cannot be separated from the history of the various stages of society. The variations in form are like variations in soil, climate, trees, vegetation. Over a long period of time, however, dance along with other arts and social functions, became integrated into the evolving hierarchical structures of society effecting a transformation in its role – from communal participation to communal consumption.

The codification of dance in a society that admitted a hierarchical structure introduced a process of rigidification in the roles of the performer and the spectator, propelling classical dance and dancers towards limiting, though exotic, specialization and to a fossilization of the form. Increasingly, the dances became a class preserve expressing an ideological content.

However, through all the distortions of the medieval period, the body retained a certain primacy and sensuality and played a vital role in maintaining human dignity in spite of much privation. It is when we come to contemporary times and an industrial/urban society that a sudden and harsh break occurs. The vital link, between body and nature, body and work, body and ritual, snaps. Dance becomes, almost totally, a spectacle.

A reversal, too, takes place. While

2 and 3
Two sequences from "Angika" choreographed by Chandralekha. This work grew out of a concern for what is happening to the human body in our times. Through this work Chandralekha explored the physical traditions like Kalaripayattu, the martial art of Kerala and its relation with the dance revealing integral relationships between principles of work, ritual, performing, eating, and healing practices, indicating the tight unity of their dynamic structures and common origins. Photographs: Dashrath Patel.

traditional thought conceptualizes the human body as a unique centre, a centre of the universe, expanding outwards into the cosmos, industrial society converts the human body into the prime target of attack: as citizen, attacked by the political system; as consumer, attacked by the economic system; as individual, bombarded by the media, denied contact with nature, incapable of self-renewal, suffocated by poisons in air and water, isolated and deprived of directions for change.

The question then arises: What role can dance play in such a society? Can it recuperate energies? Can it initiate a living flow between individual and community? Can it integrate human perspectives? Can it infuse people with joy for life, radical optimism, hope, courage, and vision to negate all that is ugly, unjust, and hurtful? If our life is alienated, can our dances and arts help to transcend that alienation?

I have experienced dance as a sensual language of beauty and of essential freedom; a language of coordination as against alienation; a movement towards the human essence, the sap, the vitality, the *rasa*. It is this aspect of classical dance and its unflagging potential to regenerate the human spirit that constitutes for me its *contemporaneity* and the reason why we need to work with the form. Any human mode with a capacity to touch, to energize, to transform is potent. Otherwise art is primarily to be lived. It is nothing but the quality of all that is made.

Besides several negative features in the prevailing dance situation like spectacular mindlessness, archaic social values, faked religiosity, idealization leading to mortification of the form, numbing sentimentality, literalism, verbalism, dependence on *sahitya*, on word, mystification and dollification, perpetuation of anti-women values, cynicism within the solo dance situation and its senseless competitiveness, there are also more serious questions: Why have classical Indian dances become so insular and unresponsive to the dramatic social, historical, scientific, human changes that have occurred in the

solutions. I believe one can make only one small step at a time with feeling and sincerity. The principles of wholeness and relatedness that form the core of traditional thought are the most relevant for us today. Through these we get some idea of the directions for a fresh search, questions of perceptual and creative levels, exchange and transmission, movement and control, art and experience, tradition and modernity, inner and outer, space and time, individual and collective, integrity and rupture, quantity and quality.

4

In "Prana", Chandralekha explores the relatedness of breath and movement; a journey towards renewal of energies, towards recovery of breath. The choreography is based on the multi-centred space concept of Navagraha iconography. Chandralekha has also used yoga movements in her choreography. Photograph: Dashrath Patel.

world around us over the past forty years? What blocks and complexes prevent classical dancers from initiating basic changes? What makes them resistant to contemporary progressive social values? Why is it that even purely formal exercises and experiments have eluded these forms? Why have not attempts been encouraged to explore the power and strength of these forms, as for example, their links with martial arts?

At the same time, the criteria, the parameters, the references, the directions for what constitutes "new" and "contemporary" in the realm of classical dance is a sensitive area and there can be no easy formulae and

With my root and training in a classical dance form like Bharata Natyam, with its ancient lineage and formal purity, I had to contend with several contradictions inherent in working within "traditional" form in a contemporary context.

I have increasingly been disturbed by current Western critical opinion which so effortlessly glamorizes and valorizes Eastern "traditions" in an uncritical manner, entirely from an "orientalist" and patronizing perspective. For us, in our Eastern contexts, both our "traditionality" and our "modernity" are complex and problematic areas which are not abstract theoretical categories but real everyday concerns – both of life and of performing arts.

If our so-called "traditions" are largely superficial post-colonial "inventions" which subsume the genuine experience and accumulation of the past, with its treasure-house of complex and holistic concepts of body/energy/aesthetics, then our so-called "modernity" has turned out to be a movement that privileged the "bourgeois" self, enabling an elite aesthetic to distort and de-eroticize the real and the liberating energies of the

5
In "Sri", Chandralekha choreographs a vision for the future. An iconic vision of woman who is auspicious, beautiful, luminous, and empowered; with multiple hands, multiple capacities, energies; a *dashabhuja* – with ten hands – who can change all space, who can charge all space. Photograph: Dashrath Patel.

6 and 7
Two sequences from "Mahakal", choreographed by Chandralekha. She observes: The dance of Time danced by Timelessness, Mahakal goes beyond linear notions of time, linked to fear, to clock and calendars and ultimate countdown to death. It celebrates the multiple and cyclic notions of time in indigenous cultures.
The sequence in figure 6 depicts love in the midst of unprecedented violence and annihilation and obliteration of Time through love.
Figure 7 suggests violence and death.
Photographs: Dashrath Patel.

body. Those of us engaged in a battle for "recovery" in several artistic and intellectual fields, therefore, find ourselves simultaneously battling on two fronts, often tending to get isolated and marginalized by national and international markets, by official state policy, and dominant cultural constructs.

If someone like me battles on regardless, it is entirely because of the pleasure I derive on the one hand from knocking the narrow-mindedness and vested interests, both at the national and international level and, on the other, from a real vision of the full blooming of a form that, I am convinced, can make a difference to the way we are looking at ourselves.

In our contexts, I believe dance is a "project" that would enable a recovery of the body, of our spine, which for me, is a metaphor for freedom. Dance, for me, is not spectacle, or entertainment, or virtuosity.

It is not about seduction or titillation or loaded effects or exotic representations. For me, it is all about evoking human energy and dignity in an increasingly brutalizing environment. Working with – and making a departure from – the exclusive classicism of Bharata Natyam, therefore, the questions before me have been: how to explore, expand, universalize the form; how to comprehend its inherent energy content; how to see it in relation to other allied physical disciplines in India – like yoga, ancient martial arts, and allied life activity with its investment in physical labour; how to interpret the purity of the Bharata Natyam line; its principles of balance and flexion; its body geometry of squares, circles, triangles, coils, curves; how to visualize this body-geometry in terms of space-geometry – the inner/outer correspondence; how to slash across the dead weight of the "past" suffocating dance in the

8
"Sharira", choreographed by Chandralekha, is about the living body without compartments – within which sexuality, sensuality, spirituality coexist, acknowledging no frontiers. Derived from the root word Sri (to rest upon or support), "Sharira" becomes the framework by means of which the self can experience the world. Photograph: Sadanand Menon.

name of "tradition"; how to pare dance of its feudal and religious acculturations, sticking like unhealthy patinas to the form, as also from the increasing pressure on it of the demands of the commercial market.

There are more questions: how to understand dance as a language in its own right, self-sufficient and with a vocabulary of its own – so as to free it from the tedious god/goddess narratives and staged religiosity, to give it a secular space of its own; how to demystify its content, which reinforces nostalgia and revivalism, promotes esoteric self-indulgence, and idealizes a deep woman content; how to recover and celebrate its abstract content of space and time; how to initiate and consolidate the conjunctions between our traditional forms and our contemporary concerns.

Any work with dance, therefore, in my context, involves engaging with the body and its primitive accumulations, its social complexes, its cultural stratifications. The "content" of the body is vast and complex. There are no limited or fragmented concepts of the body in indigenous cultures. Here, the body is seen as a unity – with respect to itself as well as the society and the cosmos. Neither specific parts of the body nor physical systems are seen in isolation. For example, the traditional martial art form Kalaripayattu, with its swift leaps and spinal stretches, is integral with a scientific understanding of secretive points in the body – such as *marma*s and *chahra*s. An ability to hurt presumes an ability to heal.

In this cosmology, the arts and sciences, too, are interdependent and richly cross-referenced. Dance, music, architecture,

sculpture, yoga, medicine, martial arts, linguistics, grammar, are not isolated and mutually exclusive. This is the larger meaning of "tradition" – to be integral, to be whole. Once this is understood, it is not "tradition" we will need to break as much as the conditions that create isolation, exclusivity, specialization, competition. It is binary categories which promote narrow beliefs and linearity, against the joys of a world-view and curvature, that we need to break.

So, with all its contradictions, conflicts, tensions, splits, and ruptures, tradition, for me, is not a museum piece or fossil form, hermetically sealed forever, which precludes ideation, commentary, questioning, critique. I see tradition as open and fluid in terms of our times, in interactive relation with the past, accepting as well as foregrounding the tensions and disjunctions. This is the only way to locate tradition here and now – as a prerequisite for renewal of our energies at the level of our everyday life.

The issue, for me, is not "tradition" versus "modernity". I do not see them as two different things. The task of the artist is to modernize the tradition through the creative process.

Not transplanting, borrowing, imitating, or becoming a "shadow culture" of some other culture. It has to be an inward journey into one's own self; a journey constantly relating, refining the reality of the in-between area; to enable tradition to flow free in our contemporary life.

Innovations in Specific Forms

innovations
in kathak

Kumudini Lakhia

I started learning dance at a very early age, long before I knew what dance was all about. The possibility that I might one day take it up as a career never occurred to my parents, whose only purpose was to make our music and dance heritage part of my education. Not until I had graduated in agriculture science did I give serious thought to dance as a career.

I went through a rather long and tedious training in Kathak in the 1940s, though I had the opportunity of learning with the best of the gurus, Guru Shambhu Maharaj and Pandit Sunder Prasad. Guru Shambhu Maharaj's approach to dance was holistic and he incorporated in his teaching a wide range of knowledge and information. Yet I had a whole lot of questions which could never be asked as in the guru-shishya parampara there is no room for questioning.

After my training I tried for some years to perform as a solo dancer. There were moments of joy but never of complete satisfaction or "ananda" as it is known in Indian aesthetics. Every artist has to have an intimate relationship with the art form which he/she practises. For me it became difficult at a point in time to build up that relationship because I could not relate to the values, thought

processes, and the attitudes of my gurus, in spite of holding them in great reverence and respect. This naturally created a state of conflict in me. I had to find a judicious balance between my sensitivity and sensibility. A dancer uses the energy of her physical body to find new expressions in dance, which may solve some of her queries. I craved to do something more and something different with the dance I knew, but did not quite know what. My first experience with how fascinating the creation process of dance can be was in 1947–52, when I was working with Ram Gopal (1912–2003), a great dancer of his time. It was because of him that I became aware of the importance of space, its potency and its flexibility. Another important thing I learnt from Ram Gopal was discipline. Discipline of time, action, and movement.

Dance and music have always gone hand-in-hand. You cannot think of one without the other. In classical Kathak, music plays a timekeeper's role in the form of a *lehara* played on the sarangi. It is only in the performance of *thumri*, *bhajan*, or *hori* that there is vocal music to which the dancer does

"Duvidha", a solo by Kumudini
Lakhia, dwelt on the conflict
between tradition and the new
and contemporary, using basic
Kathak movements.

the *abhinaya*. Creative music was never a part of Kathak. I am very fortunate to have been associated with Atul Desai, not only an excellent vocalist but also an extremely talented music composer. He trained extensively in classical Hindustani music under Pandit Omkarnath Thakur and also studied contemporary music with well-known composers of Western music. His range therefore, is very wide and highly imaginative. Working with him has been a most encouraging and positive experience.

It is not possible to work alone in the field of choreography, one has to draw in other dancers. The challenge was to train people to dance, to institutionalize the training, and to create a laboratory where ideas could shape into designs of movement. More important was my own growth as a human being and creative artist. In dance choreography there are a number of other factors which need to be coordinated, such as music, costumes, lights etc., all of which become an integral part of the choreographic process.

The concept of choreography as practised in the Western world was not prevalent in India in the 1960s. Dancers were never credited with having the ability to create or even possessing a basic intellect. They were expected to be photocopies of their gurus; unfortunately, this is still the case. Even though most of our traditional dance has been choreographed at one time or other in the past by the great masters, it is passed on to the next generation in that exact form, thus it becomes "traditional", and is accepted as the last word in terms of authenticity. Changing it would be taboo. Choreography requires the redesigning and reconstructing of the known

dance structure and space to suit the required theme and concept. Without a sound knowledge of the basic dance tradition, this can lead to sacrilege. To be able to produce a dance piece, or let us say to put it in the showroom, one has to have material in the stockroom. The source has to be ever rich. That is why I draw from my classical Kathak training which is so abundant in material. Besides sound knowledge of a particular dance discipline, the choreographer must be exposed to a wide range of experiences. It is from the depths of tensions and sorrows that the urgency to face life with new energy emerges.

I started combinations and permutations within the given structure of the Kathak technique. Once the initial fear was overcome I discovered a whole lot of new movements. How do new movements emerge? It is like asking how does a painter create a new work, how does a poet compose a new poem? It is an energy within you which sprouts in a new form and takes various shapes and shades of the discipline involved, be it painting, poetry, or dance. A single image leads to many other imaginative combinations from which you can create a whole new pattern. Take the example of clapping your hands: try and use areas around your body in the act. The movement will look different at every angle. Now try clapping in different ways, try silences between claps, then change your position – sitting down, standing up, kneeling down, standing on your toes, jumping up, turning around. You already have here a variety of material.

You can do the same kind of thing with any movement. The "pandits" may not accept them as traditional Kathak movements but what emerges from a traditional Kathak training has to be Kathak. And what I did looked like Kathak. In fact, there were many imitators.

My very first attempt at choreography was "A Variation in Thumri" in 1967. The first variation was that the *thumri* was presented by five dancers instead of the usual solo format. The visual variation came from different coloured transparent screens hung on the stage through which the dancers, dressed in white, were seen, so they took on the colours of the screens. I was thrilled at the

2
"Khunti par Tange Log" was considered a turning point in the creative *abhinaya* of Kathak.

time and so were the spectators, but looking back on the production now, it seems naïve and elementary. My personal journey through innovations in Kathak is best understood through four of my subsequent works.

"Dhabkar" (1973)

In Kathak, the technique pulsates within the human body while going through the repertoire of a performance. In the Kathak technique the word for this is *kasak-masak*. The movement starts at the wrist and the swaying of the head from the neck and the swaying of the body from the ankles, much as tall coconut trees on the seashore sway with the breeze. A student in a class is taught this without actually knowing what it is. This is the actual life-giving process of the Kathak movement which I call "Dhabkar" or pulse.

Dancers squatting at different levels of the stage and making identical movements looked different because they were seen from different angles. If the arms of one dancer gave the image of a straight line, the arms of another would look oval, those of yet another formed a circle, even though they were all in the same position. The action began in a slow tempo, gradually increasing and finally reaching a climax. This dance number also experimented with extension of movement: one single movement passing from one dancer to another giving the impression of a single movement in an extended form. There was also an attempt at breaking a pattern of movement into fragments, each performed by a different dancer. This experiment was quite new at the time in 1973 but has now become very common and imitated in Kathak. Various claims have been made for having originated it.

The music of "Dhabkar" was unique in the sense that when the dance movements were slow the music was in fast tempo, and vice versa. Even today, "Dhabkar" has a perennial quality and dancers love to perform it.

"Atah-Kim" (1981)

"Atah-Kim" means "where do we go from here?" This concept came to my mind when I was disturbed with the limitations of the presentation of Kathak technique, which had created barriers for me as a performing artist. I wanted very much to do something different. I looked at the basic postures and questioned them: why does the hand have to be exactly there, why not there, or here, or nowhere – behind the body? New ideas developed and instead of a solo dance format a group was involved in the question of "what do we do next?"

As a prop there was a frame at the centre towards the back, which symbolized my mindset at that time. Did I want to be within the frame or did I want to look at it from the outside? This was the theme. The dancers, each clamouring to get inside the frame and gain

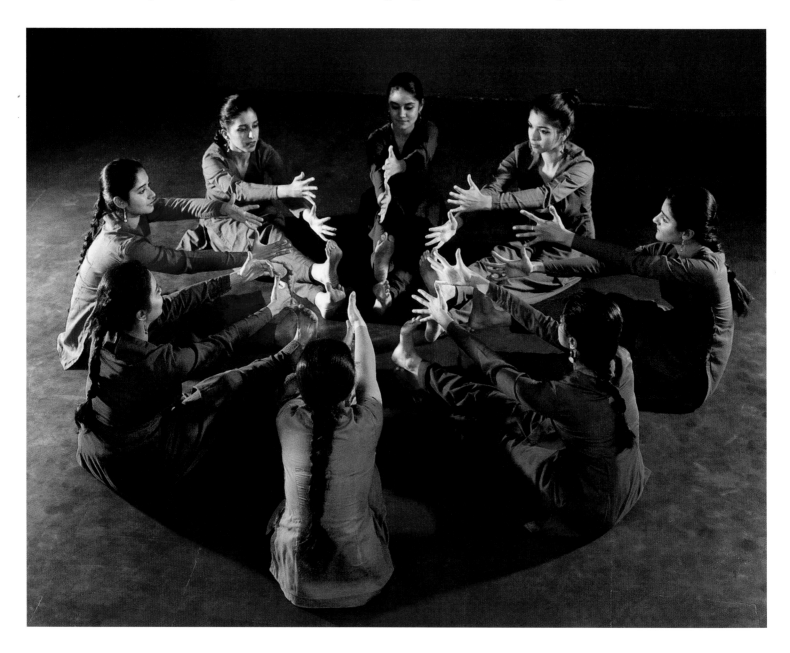

pride of place, once in, had to obey the dictates of those outside. There were confrontations, group formations, lobbying, and discordant behavioural patterns. It almost took on political colour. Being apolitical myself, this idea of image building did not occur till later in the production. Thus, sometimes one begins work with a certain idea but the end product is in a different genre. This can be a very interesting experience because it happens accidentally, without planning.

"The Coat" (Khunti par Tange Log) (1985)

Sarveshwar Dayal Saxena, the well known Hindi poet and a very dear friend of mine, once asked me if I could choreograph a piece to one of his poems. I agreed without giving it much thought. It was not the first time that dance would be related to poetry. In the Kathak technique, dancers have always danced to the words of a *thumri*, *ghazal*, *hori*, etc. But when Sarveshwar started reciting his poem, it seemed as if not a single word of it could be translated into dance language. I felt extremely jealous of the poet as he needed only a sheet of paper to write on whereas I had to create on a large scale, in a performing space. The poem was about a jacket that had

become useless with age, hanging from a peg, and its ego trips. The dust gathering on the sleeves, the buttons now broken, and the sorrow of being alone after a life of service.... How was it possible to hang from a peg these emotions so poignant?

I created the character of an alter ego whose behaviour would reflect the emotional qualities of the main character "The Coat". The conflict between two characters was more visually effective because what can be written in words cannot always be danced. The innovative quality of this production was that the expression was not word to word as is the general pattern in the classical Kathak technique, but word to mood.

When the poet spoke of dark clouds or a tree full of singing birds, these images were created by a group of dancers. The group also showed the different moods of the central character, the jacket, at times on a high, at other times very low. This production was considered a turning point in the creative *abhinaya* of Kathak.

"Sama Samvedan" (1993)

How does one live with others in society? How does one relate to other people? Past

5 (*opposite*)
In "Shravan – in Search of Sound", Kumudini had dancers in white costumes, with a white backdrop.

6
Using traditional compositions like *tarana* for *nritta*, pure dance, and using the Kathak movements, Kumudini astounded audiences with her imaginative approach, compelling the viewers' attention away from a solo dancer to the group.

moments in one's life – how do they affect one now? Does one have to waste precious time on trivialities?

For the visual format I chose a character who cannot fit into what goes on around him in his everyday life. He tries to change but the effort is too much! This was the theme of this project. While a group of dancers do formal movements in structured design, he is isolated, always trying to be part of the group, but never really succeeding. This theme demanded well defined group work. The solo character did different movements because he was at loggerheads with what was considered normal. Interrelationships between the movements of the group and the solo character could be

effective only with alternate patterns of movements, at times forceful, and at others subtle and full of emotion.

The music had the emotional quality required to portray the inner and intimate feelings of the individual as well as the chaos of the outside world. The costumes were kept simple in order that all movements be clearly seen. We used a streetlights effect rather than mood lighting to create an informal and common man's space.

***

What inspired me to look at dance in a different way was the fact that in all other art forms such as music, painting, architecture, sculpture, etc., artists were thinking progressively and their mindset was attuned with the contemporary aesthetic needs of society, some were futuristic in their approach. In dance nothing was happening. We seemed to be rooted in one place with a mutual admiration society around us. This spelt the end

of dance or at least of Kathak. Being interested in various other arts, I tried to correlate Kathak to miniature painting, the result of which was my production "Venu-Naad" in 1970; to poetry, which resulted in "The Coat"; to architecture, which was in the production "Atah-Kim" where space was used to create architectural shapes and design. Music of course is always an integral part of any production. It plays a significant role in creating the right mood and seems to complement the dance movements. I have tried to create a piece in silence but not with great success yet; maybe one day silence will be the music of a dance production.

Photo Credits
All photographs courtesy Kadamb, Centre for Dance and Music, Ahmedabad.

manipuri dances: extending the boundaries

Sunil Kothari

Geographically bounded on one side by the Indo-Burma border and on the other by the Assam Hills, Manipur has for centuries preserved and nurtured its own distinct dance and music traditions. There is no occasion during which dance and music are not a part of life in Manipur. Right from the birth of a child, the piercing of the ears, the sacred thread ceremony, marriage, death, after-death ceremonies – all the major stages of life are celebrated with dance and music. Nowhere else in India are dance and music so closely interwoven with rituals and religious practice. One rarely comes across any Manipuri (Meitei) who does not know dance and music.

In Manipur, before the advent of Vaishnavism, the Manipuri people had their own indigenous religious belief system. Even after the spread of Vaishnavism from Bengal the earlier religious beliefs and practices still prevail and are a part of their life. Raja Bhagyachandra, who ruled from 1754 to 1789 was a grandson of Garib Nawaz, who had accepted the Ramanandi faith of Vaishnavism. Bhagyachandra accepted the Gaudiya Vaishnava faith of Chaitanya Mahaprabhu. He had a dream and a vision in which the Rasa dance was revealed to him by Lord Krishna. The king introduced the Rasalila, and the earlier dance forms were metamorphosed into the highly aesthetic Rasalilas. The *kirtana*s of Bengal and other musical traditions also were introduced.

Manipur offers a staggering variety of dances: the pre-Vaishnava dance forms such as Lai Haraoba, the dance of Maibas and Maibis, the priests and priestesses; the Pung Cholom (playing on the cylindrical drums while dancing); Karatala Cholom (playing cymbals and dancing, clap dance); Natasankirtan, in which men perform Karatala Cholom, Pung Cholom, and sing and dance, before the Rasalilas; Nupi Khubak Ishei, in which women sing in a very high pitch, indulge in repartee and dance, and so on. Besides this there is a vibrant tradition of Thang-ta, the martial art of Manipur, wielding sword and spear, practised by both men and women.

When Rabindranath Tagore saw Manipuri dances for the first time at Silchar, he arranged for its teaching by inviting traditional gurus to Viswabharati, the university he had established in Santiniketan. The technique of Manipuri was also employed for the dance-dramas he wrote and for which he also wrote the music. This was the beginning of traditional Manipuri dances finding another arena than mere traditional performances in Manipur. When Nabhakumar Singh went to Ahmedabad and Guru Bipin Singh to Bombay, Manipuri found another venue in the metropolitan cities. Guru Amubi Singh was invited by no less a choreographer and brilliant dancer than Uday Shankar to his Almora dance centre. Guru Amubi Singh's association with Uday Shankar brought happy results with the choreography of the film *Kalpana*, dovetailing Manipuri dances with contemporary sensibilities. Whereas Guru Bipin Singh with his disciples the four Jhaveri Sisters embarked upon experimentations within the tradition – expanding the classical language, creating solos, duets, group dances, with complex *tala*s and correlating the *Natyashastra*, Bengali *kavya*, and *shastra* texts to the classical Manipuri dances, artists like Rajkumar Singhjit Singh who moved to New Delhi, invested the tradition with metropolitan sensibilities and created ballets of lasting beauty using diverse Manipuri forms at Triveni Kala Sangam in that city.

Beginning with the first full-length Manipuri ballet "Babruvahan", using different aspects of the dance form, including Jagoi,

1
R.K. Singhjit Singh, with his wife Charu Sija, used diverse Manipuri forms in his full-length ballets. A sequence from "Leiman", Discarded Flower, in which she sees her beloved for the last time. Photograph: R.K. Singhjit Singh.

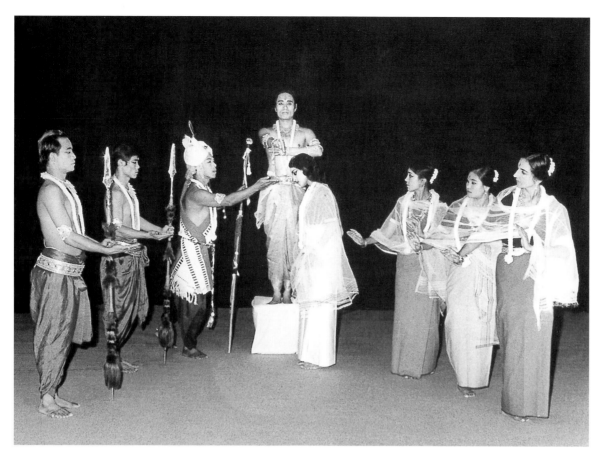

2
A sequence from "Ingel-Lei".
Ingel-Lei represents the gentle
spirit which tames the river in
spate. But the tragedy is that
to stop the devastation she
must be sacrificed. Photograph:
R.K. Singhjit Singh.

3
The injustice suffered by Sita
finds felicitous interpretation
in this Ramayana ballet
produced and choreographed
by R.K. Singhjit Singh. Here,
Hanumana the messenger from
Rama arrives at Ashok Vatika
where Sita is held captive.
Photograph: Sanjay Kumar.

SUNIL KOTHARI

Cholom, and Thang-ta, Singhjit Singh continued to produce one ballet after another each year, totalling more than 35, with themes from Manipuri legends like "Hayloee", "Ingel-Lei", "Leiman Khamba Thoibi", as well as stories from the Indian epics including "Shakuntala", "Savitri", "Seeta", and "Kumarasambhava".

He also choreographed ballets using abstract themes like "Maya", "Kalachakra", "Chhaya Purush", and "Suvarna Dweep". After leaving Triveni Kala Sangam both Singhjit Singh and his wife Charu Sija (nee Mathur) have continued choreographing works which reflect contemporary sensibilities as seen in the latest production "Nupi Lan" by Charu Sija and "Search" by Singhjit Singh. From the sets, the costumes, the lighting, the dance, to the music, their choreographic works have consistently shown high aesthetic standards in all departments.

In Manipur the dancers and the choreographers Rajkumar Priyagopalasana and Th. Tarunkumar Singh were busy bringing in the advantages of their experiences and exposure on account of their travels abroad and within India in terms of presentation and choreography. Priyagopalasana visited Mumbai and also travelled extensively abroad with Louise Lightfoot, the Australian dancer and choreographer. Tarunkumar with his wife Bilasini Devi had performed and travelled in

4
In ballets like "Chhaya Purush", R.K. Singhjit Singh explores the abstract theme of the darker side of human nature. Unbridled greed for more power finally leads to man's own destruction by the dark manifestation he himself has cultivated. Photograph: Sanjay Kumar.

5
In "Nupi Lan", Women's Struggle, the choreographer Charu Sija deals with the woman power that surfaces to save their families from starvation and exploitation. They fight against the menace of drugs smuggling to which the young fall victim. Photograph: Avinash Pasricha.

different parts of the country under the banner of Haren Ghosh Impresario.

After independence, when the Jawaharlal Nehru Manipur Dance Academy (JNMDA) was established in 1954 at Imphal, regular training in various aspects of Manipuri dance traditions was systematized. Since 1975 it also has a Production Unit. It has to date produced 27 dance-dramas, with five outstanding works, choreographed by Priyagopalasana: "Kabui Kei

A major breakthrough came with young Th. Chaotombi choreographing "Keibul Lamjao" in 1984–85. It dealt with the floating sanctuary around Loktak lake, the home of the sangai, brow-antlered deer, which is currently in serious danger of extinction. Written by Raj Kumari Binodini Devi, the renowned Sahitya Akademi Award winner, it expresses this anxiety and the vision of the elegant dancing sangais. It is an attempt to represent the

6 (*opposite*)
R.K. Singhjit Singh and Charu Sija in a traditional duet. Photograph: Avinash Pasricha.

7
A sequence from "Keibul Lamjao", choreographed by Th. Chaotombi dealing with the theme of sangai, deer currently in danger of extinction. This ballet achieved a major breakthrough in terms of kinetic movement and also thematic content. Photograph courtesy Th. Chaotombi Singh, Jawaharlal Nehru Manipur Dance Academy, Imphal.

Oiba", "Mangsat", "Rajashri Bhagyachandra", "Nongpok Panthoibi", and "Chaitanya Mahaprabhu"; two by Tarunkumar Singh: "Nongdol Leima" and "Sarik Makhol"; three by Babu Singh: "Ramayana", "Loktak Ishei", and "Bashak Leela", and a majority of the recent works by Th. Chaotombi Singh and a few by W. Lokendrajit Singh. However, in terms of thematic content these dance-dramas abound in mythological stories, local legends, and folk tales. They do not address contemporary issues.

appeal for protecting wildlife. A contemporary issue related to preservation of wildlife in its treatment through a fable, innovative technique, dancing, costumes, humans playing the roles of dancing deer, and music with imaginative choreography, it is a benchmark in the dance-dramas so far produced. When it was presented at the Nritya-Natika Festival of the Sangeet Natak Akademi in Delhi, it was received warmly, winning praise for furthering the boundaries of Manipuri dance.

8–10
In "Keibul Lamjao", the development of
the story to imaginative choreography,
sets, costumes, and music leaves an
indelible impression. A documentary
has been made of this ballet.
Photographs courtesy Th. Chaotombi
Singh, Jawaharlal Nehru Manipur
Dance Academy, Imphal.

11 and 12
Priti Patel explores
contemporary issues through
Manipuri dance traditions in
her choreographic creations
like "Malem (Prithvi – Earth)".
Photographs: Satyaki Ghosh.

Another dance-drama "Ballad of Loktak" written by Binodini Devi and choreographed by Babu Singh, also finds felicitous expression of concern for the environment. It incorporated the poem "On Loktak Edge" by Khwairakpam Chaoba and the tongue-in-cheek poem about the much developed Loktak lake in the poem "Loktak Project" by contemporary poet Laishram Somorendra. Both dance-dramas "Kaibul Lamjao" and "Ballad of Loktak" stand out for their thematic content and commensurate Manipuri technique. Doubtless these productions have extended the boundaries of Manipuri dance in seeking new directions.

In recent years Priti Patel, a former disciple of Guru Bipin Singh has made her presence felt on the national and international dance scene with her choreographic works dealing with themes which are different from mythology and legends. She has also explored the martial arts of Manipur taking assistance from a group of male dancers and drummers, the pung players, using also the drum traditions.

Exploring the traditions of Rasalila, Natasankirtan, Thang-ta, and Lai Haraoba, Priti has in her choreographic works like "Malem (Prithvi – Earth)", interpreted the content by suggesting that though the Earth is our mother who gives us everything, we use her as a commodity and there is no end to man's greed. In "Suryagati", Priti explores the movement of the sun from morning to evening, which has special significance in Manipuri tradition, with ritualistic Thang-ta and Rasalila techniques in different contexts, not in the usual context of Rasalila. Such departures offer new insights and extend the frontiers of the technique. A contemporary poem by Somorendra Singh "Olive Green" deals with the present plight of Manipur, the constant presence of soldiers in olive green uniform, in contrast to the glory of the rising sun and the blooming of beautiful orchids, depicting the troubled times.

The same agony is seen in "Khuman" (Black Sun). The land of seven clans and man's paradise has been torn asunder with struggle and strife for years. Young boys have been dying for a cause, simply to be heard and to be understood. Rasalilas and Natasankirtan transport the dancer from the reality of killing and bloodshed, bomb blasts and gunshots, to the world of Krishna who fights demons and who mesmerizes gopis in the night-long dance-dramas. But one has to wake up from this fantasy to face the reality of the bombs and the guns as gifts of the present century. These dance forms, an integral part of the lives of Manipur's people, are going through the same crisis. The commentary in English translation helps convey the poignancy of the present situation in Manipur.

In a recent production "Nahal Nong" (Once Upon a Time), choreographed by Priti Patel, the jealous brother's attempts to destroy the earth are challenged by Nongthang Leina, the goddess of lightning, a metaphor for female force, who succeeds in creating the earth anew. Using huge drums and state-of-the-art technology, the dancers descending on the stage in a contraption, Priti Patel and her team of Thang-ta dancers and drummers invest Manipuri dance tradition with a

13
In "Suryagati", Priti Patel deals with the movement of the sun, using Thang-ta and Rasalila techniques in different contexts. Such departures offer new insights and extend the frontiers of the technique. Photograph: Satyaki Ghosh.

contemporary kinetic language with which audiences are able to identify.

From the stories of the gods and goddesses to stories of the people, Manipuri dances have made a long journey and with the emergence of young choreographers the boundaries of Manipuri dances are being extended. No longer do dancers shy away from deviating from the tradition, but they boldly attempt to bring in elements of martial arts which quicken the pace and invest the form with a pulsating, throbbing, vital element. No one now thinks of Manipuri dances as slow-paced, flowing, meandering, and gentle; instead we marvel at their ability to adapt to changes reflecting contemporary sensibilities. Whereas in villages one often sees night-long performances of Rasalilas, one is equally impressed by the bold experiments which exist side by side with the traditional performances. This has helped Manipuri dances keep pace with the changing times.

navanritya – a contemporary methodology: history, theory, practice

Ranjabati Sircar

In 1983 Dancers' Guild was founded in Calcutta by my mother, Dr Manjusri Chaki Sircar. She had been living abroad for almost twenty years, in Africa and the United States, and had decided to return to India to explore some of the ideas she had evolved as a choreographer. I myself had been in India for four years already, continuing the dance studies begun as a child under her guidance with other gurus, pursuing academics, and having my first experience of India on my own after a childhood spent abroad. My mother's return to India put her work into a new perspective for me to recognize its innovativeness in the context of Indian dance, and I decided to work with her. I suggested the name "Dancers' Guild" as the name for our company.

In the early years when I worked as Principal Dancer and Assistant Choreographer, apart from being in charge of most secretarial, public relations, and administrative aspects of the company, my role was to some degree one of transliterator and interpreter. As a dancer, I was called upon to interpret songs, poetry, characters, and abstractions, while as an assistant I was constantly exploring movement and making suggestions in the choreography. Within a year, I realized that the amount of material being amassed needed some sort of order, and that such an order would be useful in communicating with other dancers and, particularly, in transmitting ideas to new dancers. This material went back many years to various experimentations explored by Manjusri since her college years, and was growing constantly. I began to explore various avenues of classifying the material we had already created. The modes of classification in the classical forms I had been studying were not helpful; they did not seem to have any obvious logic, which I felt would be important

1
Ranjabati Sircar as Prakriti in "Tomari Matir Kanya", choreographed by Manjusri Chaki Sircar. Photograph: Avinash Pasricha.

for our work. It was also clear that classification according to form (i.e., movements derived from Bharata Natyam, movements derived from Kathakali, etc.) would be counterproductive to the basic effort, which was to evolve a contemporary language of dance based on traditional forms but free from their intrinsic boundaries. After a great deal of thought, discussions with different gurus including my own, and reading about other training methodologies, I came up with the idea of classification according to the relationship of the body to space and its shape in that space.

I began to discuss this with Manjusri and the dancers to find out if there was any obvious grouping according to the kinds of movements we worked with, and soon discovered that all our movement could be classified under eight categories, to which Manjusri gave Sanskrit names, as follows:

1. *Bhumisparsha*: floor-touching movements. The body is sitting or lying on the floor.

2. *Madhyabhangi*: middle-level movements. The body is in full mandala position, hips resting on one or both heels, one or both knees fully flexed.

3. *Sthanaka*: standing positions. Important to understand the different qualities

of stance derived from different traditional forms.

    4. *Tribhanga*: three-bend positions, both static and moving. An important variation existent in nearly all traditional forms and an important source for a variety of movements.

    5. *Chalana*: movements covering space. Including falling, rolling, tumbling, as well as any kind of walking or running movement.

    6. *Urdhvagati*: upward movements. The leg is extended above waist-level.

    7. *Ullamphana*: jumping movements.

Both feet leave the floor, at the same time or one following the other.

    8. *Bhangisamashti*: clustered positions, both static and moving. Two or more bodies create a pattern.

For the eight groups I suggested the name Navanritya, indicating the idea of a new way of seeing, a new approach to movement and choreography. The eight groups each have particular warming-up and development methods designed to prepare the body for movement. Students are expected to have prior training in classical dance, or to have some background of movement such as yoga or martial arts; the method of teaching is largely through analytical understanding, so they must be of a certain age, and classical training prior to this has been found useful as a prerequisite.

The period 1983-90 saw several works choreographed by Manjusri employing this approach and also serving as groundwork for the evolution of the various groups of movement. "Tomari Matir Kanya", "Chitrangada", "Raag o Rupantar", "Sri o Shakti", "Juddher Damama", and "Nrityakatha Mirabai" all belong to this period. During the period 1990-98, the work expanded with my joining my mother as Co-Director of Dancers' Guild, and choreographing with her "Aranya-Amrita", "Tasher Desh", and "Charaiboti". Manjusri also worked individually with the group on "Kraunchakatha", "Yugasandhi", "Parama-Prakriti", and "Shei Meye", while I created the solo works "Gangavataran", "Fable for La Gran Sabana", "Wandering Songs", and "Cassandra", focusing on a deeper, more individual exploration of movement and emotion. This was also the period in which I extended the Navanritya base to work in collaboration with artists of different training backgrounds, in "Ice and Fire", "Meeting Jhulan", and "La Terre Blessee", and to choreograph for dancers based in the UK, in "Thirsting River" and "Oblique", as well as in Senegal for the Dancers' Guild company, exploring wit, celebration, and humour. We both had the opportunity to work with composers, musicians, designers, and artists who added to the expansion of our work on a variety of levels.

As I taught in many workshops around the world, I found increasingly that Navanritya was a highly efficient method of training dancers in various forms of movement derived from the Indian base, even if their original training was in completely different forms. From colleagues of different backgrounds and in different parts of the world, I received the affirmation that they found the method of deconstructing traditional movements and applying them in new contexts very useful. An important aspect of the methodology is the incorporation of *abhinaya* techniques, as a source of motivation. The movements learned are never seen as purely physical, but are related to situations, feelings, and impulses within the same pattern and evolve different dynamics. Similarly, an emotional impulse may be the source of a movement, and serve as the root of various kinds of development. One of my own specializations in Navanritya has been deconstructing *abhinaya* as learned under Shrimati Kalanidhi Narayanan.

While at first, dancers are encouraged to recognize the root sources of movement, and to identify the varying differences in weight,

shape, dynamic, and impetus that give a movement its particular stylistic flavour, with further training they are discouraged from making this connection except in reference to particular lines or positions of the body that

articulate technique. Movements within the groups thus take on various referential names, which help in indicating a root (already removed from its source) that can then be explored and further developed. In the case of individual movement, dancers are continually coming up with new variations and improvisations based on their own exploration of the root movements and positions. In my own case, I work directly with the abstract quality of a movement, completely ignoring its traditional source. The question may arise: how are all these movements, of various sources, connected within the body? The preparation work on centring may hold the answer; so may various techniques of breathing which are explored in the context of movement and transitions.

4 and 5
Ranjabati in a solo work, "The Fable for La Gran Sabana", choreographed by her. Photographs: Avinash Pasricha.

Navanritya is linked historically to Rabindranath Tagore's ideas on dance in India, which he was never able to fully develop in his lifetime. Manjusri's early work, during her college years, was centred around the songs and poetry of Tagore, through her collaborations with Debabrata Biswas, noted exponent and performer of Tagore's songs. She found a supportive and challenging platform at Presidency College, Calcutta, in the mid-1950s, and an able mentorship from Professor Debipada Bhattacharya there, and developed a team of artists all seeking expression beyond classical boundaries even as she was studying classical forms. Reviews were undertaken by fellow scholars in the college magazines, which were of a totally different ilk to the usual newspaper columns. Manjusri's year was the second year of women at Presidency, and they were already creating waves in Calcutta society by working shoulder to shoulder with their male classmates.

During her years abroad Manjusri developed solo presentations drawing more and more from her classical training (Bharata Natyam, Odissi, and Manipuri). In the early 1970s she directed a company of Indian and American dancers in New York, The Collective Dance Theatre. During this period (1968–80) she also taught regular private classes, courses at the State University of New York, and over two hundred workshops all over the United States, and began to develop the fundamentals of teaching that later evolved into Navanritya.

6-8
Ranjabati in a sequence from "Cassandra",
a solo choreographed by her. Photographs:
Avinash Pasricha.

Her inspiration was in Tagore's conviction that it was important, as a modern being, to find "our dance"; a form not following classical styles or contents but derived from them, a form capable of expressing modern concerns. As part of his search he brought many classical and folk dancers to Santiniketan, and sent students to other parts of the world. His most emphatic approval was for a choreography of his highly abstract

Tagore's philosophy. His belief in spiritual humanism sought a deeply spiritual connection with the environment and the self, beyond the boundaries of patriarchal mythologies and classical *nayika*s. Manjusri was inspired by his delineations of the modern heroines Shyama, Chandalika, Srimati, and Chitrangada to seek new ways of expressing the concerns of this philosophy, particularly as a woman. While she referred constantly to

poem "Jhulan" created by Srimati Tagore after she had studied with Mary Wigman, Kurt Joss, and Rudolf Laban. His daughter-in-law Protima Devi, a painter and choreographer, had studied at Dartington Hall, soon after its founding by the Elmhirsts on the lines of

classical forms for technique, she was also plagued by the need to simply do what the body wanted to do naturally, uninhibited by any styles. Dissatisfied both by the style of Uday Shankar and what was on offer at Santiniketan as "Rabindrik" dance, she was

9 and 10
Sequences from "Kon Nutaneri
Dak" based on "Tasher Desh",
choreographed by Ranjabati.
Photographs courtesy Dancers'
Guild, Kolkata.

convinced that she had to find her own way, particularly after seeing a performance of Martha Graham in Calcutta in the 1950s. Twenty years of living in New York and constant exposure to the best in world dance led her to realize the strength of the traditional forms as underpinnings for any modern exploration.

In formulating the Navanritya methodology, the intention has been to develop a way of training dancers so they would be able to expand beyond the boundaries of form and create bodies and minds that would be open to multifarious methods of work. To this end, the company dancers were also exposed to many other ways of working, from around India and abroad. Workshops have been hosted by the company with artists of Thang-ta, Kalaripayattu, Chhau, and Kandyan (Sri Lankan) dance traditions, as well as with artists of American and European modern dance methodologies, African dance, South American, and Native American dance forms, and those of China and Southeast Asia. The process has been one of continual opening, with the base reference point remaining the classical principles of movement, line, energy, emotion, and body embedded in the Navanritya methodology. To this end there has been no effort to develop any critical standards beyond that of "skilful communication". In the last fifteen years of Dancers' Guild's evolution, there has been constant debate as to the critical aspect of contemporary dance. Our position has always been one of openness, in keeping with the spirit of dialogue and discourse intrinsic to the contemporary arena. The final reference point for us has been Martha Graham's famous words, "Ultimately, there are only two kinds of dance: good dance and bad dance." This dictum has been a good reference point in an atmosphere in which, at times, concepts have been blocking the way of pure, un-preconditioned "seeing" of a work. Conceptual issues have their importance in developing a mental approach that is outside of the classical format, but cannot constitute a new, just as rigid, format for understanding new work. This would be nearly classicism, a kind of contemporary *Natyashastra*. In the context of the many different kinds of work that are evolving in India, there is a need for the basic tenets of post-modernism – the absence of closures, and the openness of dialogue – to be the primary factors in viewing a work. The Guild's efforts have always been to keep these doors open, to link work with historicity and sociopolitical reality, and position varieties of work in the vast arena of Indian and international contemporary dance.

An important aspect of the Navanritya methodology is the development of social awareness and political consciousness. Deconstruction of the classical and traditional dance ideologies reveals oppression of women, casteism, class exploitation, and patriarchal Brahmanic discrimination. New-colonialism and neo-imperialism pressure the dance economy to remain in a self-contained bubble of nostalgia for the exotic and the pseudo-erotic, thinly disguised by a veil of religiosity. In such an atmosphere, we feel it is vital for dancers to develop a true sense of the modern Indian self which is not defined by imported discourses, whether intellectual or touristic. This is, I believe, of vital importance when the entire idea of contemporaneity tends to be seen as a Western one. A historical perspective on Indian contemporary dance reaffirms the roots of modernity in India and gives us our own sense of "where we are coming from", beyond theories and concepts. From this point, it is possible then to "let go of concepts".

Theoretically, however, Navanritya questions the ability of ancient tools to express modern concerns. The challenge before the contemporary dancer of today is not to utilize classical forms efficiently towards contemporary expression, but to recreate the very language of dance from its roots: the roots being of vital importance, to give grounding and grammar to such expression.

Editor's Note
This article was written in 1998. Sadly, Ranjabati passed away soon after. The Navanritya tradition is being carried on by dancers from the Dancers' Guild, Kolkata.

PERSONAL EXPERIMENTS

search for
my tongue

Daksha Sheth

I was trained in Kathak by Kumudini Lakhia for eighteen years and was a member of the troupe of dancers with which she experimented in creating new directions in group choreography in Kathak. I owe a lot to her for putting me on the right path, though I had to struggle greatly to express myself in a dance vocabulary other than Kathak. When I look back on this "search for my tongue", I see three distinct phases during which I have created several choreographic works.

Early Experiments

I moved from Ahmedabad to New Delhi in 1983 to study Kathak with Birju Maharaj and Mayurbhanj Chhau with Krishna Chandra Naik. The same year I met and married Devissaro, an Australia-born musician, composer, and photographer. He was originally trained as a classical pianist and studied Dhrupad vocal music, Hindustani instrumental music for flute, and percussion pakhavaj. All my innovative works from that time on were created in artistic collaboration with Devissaro, who provided music and visual direction.

"Summer", choreographed to the music of *The Four Seasons* by the Italian composer Vivaldi was an attempt to juxtapose classical

Kathak technique with Western music. In terms of movement language it was an exploration of variations of pirouettes. It upset the traditional exponents and I was blacklisted from performing in the Kathak festival where I had premiered the work. Only recently, several years later, I was invited to present it in a Kathak festival at Kolkata featuring innovations in Kathak. This seven-minute-long work took three months to choreograph, and is still in my repertoire.

With my first experiment, it was as if a door was slammed in my face. However, when one door closes, another opens and with my forays in Chhau I discovered a new kinetic language that brought a change in my career as a classical Kathak dancer. I was one of the first women performers in the male dominated world of Chhau. I choreographed a traditional number, "Mahisasurmardini" using Devi shlokas to music by Devissaro, extending its duration to 25 minutes. Another piece I choreographed was "Kaliyamardan" with two male dancers, an unusual trio performance.

It was in "Chhaya", a duet with Vishwakant Singh, that we explored

1 and 2
Two sequences from "Yajna",
choreographed by Daksha
Sheth.

96

A scene from "Falling Angels", a collaborative work with The Kosh, a dance theatre company from London.

3 (*opposite*)
"Yajna": the third section Ahuti, where Agni is invoked. Daksha used a circle of fire against which a duet was performed, with striking visual effect.

possibilities of shadows projected on bamboo screens, using Chhau dance language and original music by Devissaro. It continued the journey of developing a unique body language from Chhau. It indeed met with critical success, enabling me to carry on my experimental works.

However, the most exciting choreographic work was "Time Piece". I was invited by Rajeev Sethi to create a "work on site" for the inauguration of the Titan watch factory. The structure was in four parts, representing different time frames: Cosmic Time, Solar Time, Life Time, and Modern Times, the latter being a Chaplinesque "day in the life...". Each section was performed on a separate level.

"Cosmic Time", which began with a "Big Bang", was performed on the roof of the factory, at a height of over twelve metres. I had to dance on a narrow platform at the very edge of the wall, else I would not be seen by the audience. Thus I was a small figure at the top of a white wall with the expanse of sky as my backdrop. The tremendous sense of risk focused the audience's attention and magnified me more effectively than any spotlight!

I danced "Solar Time" along a narrow ledge that ran the full width of the wall about 2 metres below the top. I held props showing the sun and the moon, and movements of the planets. From this level I had to descend by means of a flying fox specially built by the engineers at the factory. I sat like a goddess in a harness and flew down the wire and came to a halt at the next level, at a height of less than 3 metres.

In "Life Time" cloth was the prop. Devissaro had used pieces from Bach's Unaccompanied Cello Suites superimposed with background voices, beginning with baby voices for the childhood section moving on to voices of children playing. For the adult section, the music was by Phillip Glass. The old age section had the writer Ved Mehta's mother Amiji's voice.

"Modern Times" used Keith Jarrett's improvised piano music. Later on I developed this section into an independent number. "Modern Times" was a playful but deliberate attempt to break all the norms of dance in India. I added funny and frivolous elements – baggy pants, patchwork clothes, funky umbrella – and walked like Chaplin. Indian dancers generally do not go on stage wearing shoes, but I used Rajasthani chappals with rupee coins attached to the bottom to produce a tap sound. I sat cross-legged on a chair, concealed behind *The Times of India*, which I was reading. And the first thing which emerged from behind the newspaper was a pair of shoes, not my head. It was a tongue-in-cheek exercise in sacrilege, deliberately making fun of the established norms. The music had a fast and precise rhythm, and this number combined rhythmic exploration with light-hearted theatre.

The Vrindaban Phase

In 1989, at the invitation of Protima Bedi, Devissaro and I moved to Nrityagram near Bangalore, winding up our affairs in New Delhi. We were the first artists to stay with

5 and 6
In "Sarpagati", Daksha explored through the use of Kalaripayattu, geometrical patterns to form the square using four dancers, clad in loin cloths. Their dark bodies and powerful movements exuded sensuality/sexuality, symbolic of the serpent.

her. Then in 1990 we moved back north to Vrindaban, where we rented a large haveli, which we planned to make into a centre for creative experimentation in dance. This attempt failed, largely because we were obviously badly out of sync with the times. We thought other dancers with a passion to experiment would join us, but it did not happen.

Vrindaban offered another line of dance research to rediscover Kathak as a temple dance. With support from the Department of Culture I was able to employ local musicians and a poet, Kalyanji Prasad Sharma. Over a period of three years we created and offered dance as Nritya Seva in Radha Raman and other temples of this Braj region and we were known as the Nritya Seva Mandali.

We created "Govindalila" and "Ashtayam". The former was performed by fire light for the 500th anniversary of Govindadev temple and has been recorded by the Indira Gandhi National Centre for the Arts, New

Delhi. "Ashtayam" is a collection of compositions arranged according to the eight divisions of the day as followed in the Radha Raman temple. The poems of Ashtachhap poets were set to Haveli Sangeet, using sixteen ragas and several *tala*s. The singing has the quality of strength and rawness of the Braj region. I like it very much in contrast to the singing used in Kathak.

Then at Vrindaban arrived Simon Dove from London to invite us to the Vivarta Festival to be held in September 1992 at The Place Theatre, London. Because we could not find dancers interested in working with us in an experimental context, we turned to actors, and thus "Yajna" our major choreographic work became an experiment in the interface of dance and theatre. It included dancer Kamaljeet, actors Atul Kumar and Sheeba Chadha. "Yajna" was inspired by Vedic rites, myths, and chanting. It broadly mirrored the structure of the Vedic fire sacrifice or *yajna*. It was in three sections.

In the first section, "Elements of the Sacrifice", we explored ritual space, ritual speech, and ritual actions. It commenced with the demarcation and purification of space as preparatory to empowerment, followed by an invocation to the four directions and to sacred speech. We further explored it along with the basic geometric elements of line, the square and the diagonal.

In the second section, "Invocation of the Gods", the major Vedic deities like Varuna, the

7 and 8
"Sarpagati": sequences showing
Isha Sharvani and Anil Kumar, and
Madhu Gopinath and Daksha
Sheth executing the slow, silken,
slithering, winding and unwinding
serpent movements in a
breathtaking manner.

100

9

"Sarpagati": yoni/lingam geometric formations by Madhu Gopinath and Daksha Sheth created strong visuals, exuding sensuality/sexuality, depicting Kundalini Shakti and the ascending cycle of energy.

life. Symbolically by offering various substances to the fire, the sacrificer is offering himself as the sacrifice. Through this symbolic entering into death comes rebirth and liberation.

The text was adapted by Devissaro from the *Rigveda*, translated by Wendy O'Flaherty. The music, design, and direction were by Devissaro.

"Yajna" was subsequently produced in three versions. The original was in English, and later we had a Hindi version. Finally a Malayalam version was created when we shifted to Trivandrum in 1993.

The Trivandrum Phase

"Yajna" was a landmark in my career. The Malayalam version was scripted by Paul Zacharia, a well known writer from Trivandrum. The music combined Vedic chanting, drumming, and original music by Devissaro. "Yajna" taught us more than any other work we have choreographed.

We worked towards establishing Natyashram, a rural arts centre in lush, sylvan surroundings on the banks of Lake Vellayani, 14 kilometres from Trivandrum. It is now the permanent base of our Academy for Arts Research, Training and Innovation (Aarti). Aesthetically designed using low-cost rural technology, it provides accommodation and work areas where artists of different disciplines, cultures, and backgrounds can come together, interact, and pursue collaborative productions.

I turned to learning Indian martial arts traditions, especially Kalaripayattu, as a foundation for choreographic extension and for evolving a training methodology for the

guardian of the cosmic order, Usha, the goddess of dawn, driving the chariot of Surya, who is the celestial fire, and others are invoked.

In the third section "Ahuti" or the Oblation, Agni, god of fire, child of the waters, is of all the gods the one most accessible to man. Agni acts as a link between man and the gods, earth and sky. In rainfall, Agni again returns to the earth. Thus fire and water become a potent symbol of the cycle of dancers of my company. Devissaro and I drew on the wealth of these traditions including yoga, mallkhamb, and gymnastics. We also began to train dancers in a diverse range of musical instruments.

The Past Decade

From 1993 onwards, my gypsy life ended. With my daughter Isha Sharvani and son Tao, who are grown up and now also perform with us, in a way we have got settled. The works "Silence is a Rhythm Too", "Search for My Tongue", "Rachana", "Sangeetam", "Falling Angels", and "Sarpagati" were choreographed during this period of eight years and The Daksha Sheth Dance Company has participated in several national and international dance festivals.

The Vivarta Dance Festival commissioned a collaborative work with London-based contemporary dancer Ellen van Schulenburch. I choreographed a solo for her. Another commissioned work followed from YUVA Company, London for five British dancers titled "Tongues Untied", which I choreographed later on for my company as

10
"Sarpagati": Daksha as Golden Garuda. Both Garuda and the serpent are regarded as guardians of spiritual knowledge. Garuda as the serpent eater represents the higher consciousness.

11
"Sarpagati": Daksha explored the mallkhamb tradition; Isha Sharvani and Anil Kumar balance themselves along a rope.

"Search for My Tongue", based on a bilingual poem by Gujarati poet Sujata Bhatt, educated in the USA and now living in Germany. It deals with the dilemma of Asian youth raised in the West, caught between two cultures, their search for their identity being mirrored by the search for a mother tongue long atrophied from disuse. Through dreams and memories, and through communications with relatives in India, a vital link is forged, and with it a sense of wholeness and identity.

I saw it as cultural dislocation and transformation that our own country India is going through. And it is a metaphor for my own search for an independent dance identity and language. I have explored martial arts, Chhau technique, Kathak and Bharata Natyam rhythms, brought in elements of games and joy in my choreography experimenting with lighting and music and costumes. The young boys wear the ubiquitous trousers and T-shirts, enabling audiences to identify with the performers.

An Indo-Finnish collaborative project with composer Eero Hameenniemi, who created music for my company, gave me the scope to choreograph a work to specially composed music, with dancers exploring various movements, including Kathak rhythms, playing upon the body the *tala* patterns, ending with a joyous finale. Titled "Sangeetam", the work was set to a *tala* of fifteen beats in which song, percussion, music, and dance were united as per the definition of

Sangeetratnakara. It was performed in Helsinki.

"Falling Angels" was an Indo-British dance-theatre production between The Kosh of London and my company, initiated and funded by the British Council as part of the celebration of fifty years of Indian Independence. Though it was a genuine collaboration, the final product was neither like our work nor like theirs. This experiment failed and we took it in our stride.

Finally I come to "Sarpagati" – The Way of the Serpent – in which the theme is inspired by the significance of the snake in Indian culture. In five sections: Kundalini, Earth, Water, Fire, and Garuda, it deals with the awakened *kundalini*, the serpent energy; the earth element depicted in Tantra by a

movements, looking beyond the conventional dance movements for my choreography.

My exploration of physicality in dance, with contact between male and female dancers and the bold treatment of sensuality, shocked many traditional viewers and conservative audiences. However, it struck a chord with urban youth and later even received acceptance from diehard traditionalists. The music too was explorative with Tibetan bowls, Australian didgeridoo, the Indian bamboo flute, the rain stick from South America, wooden blocks, clapping sticks, and drums, that added several sound textures.

In this journey where do I stand now?

The most important event has been the entry of our daughter Isha Sharvani into the dance world in August 1998. In this I see a continuity in the journey I began long ago.

People may ask where is my signature in my work?

Each of my choreographic works has reflected an evolving dance vocabulary, and this evolution is the signature of my work. However eclectic my works appear, there is growth. The deviations and surprise turns in my dance career do not permit critics and viewers to pigeonhole me and my works with convenient labels. I have courage and faith in my intuition and I believe I have stretched the boundaries of Indian dance, exploring a wide range of movement idioms, performing in diverse styles. My life is driven by a passion for dance that has subsumed all other considerations. My search is continuous.

Photo Credits
All photographs by Devissaro, courtesy Daksha Sheth Dance Company.

yellow square, metaphysically representing spatial extension – length and breadth (to depict this I have used Kalaripayattu exercise positions to form a square); water, depicted by the white crescent of the second chakra – suggesting balance and flow, metaphysically representing an act of creation, in which I have used body contact, male and female, with entwining and slithering movements, female energy coiling around and activating the dormant male principle, represented by the lingam; fire, associated with the third chakra, represented by the red triangle, symbolizing both intensity and power, the drive to conquer and dominate transforming into creative energy; and finally Garuda, the enemy of the serpent – from death of the lower self, the serpent is transformed into a golden bird, and with the birth of compassion, the path of the higher chakras commences. I have used rope gymnastics for movement sequences, together with yoga and indigenous traditional

re-membering
"winds of shiva"

Uttara Asha Coorlawala

My attempt here is to look holistically backwards through recent theoretical concepts at a collaborative choreographic work titled "Winds of Shiva" and issues related to it. I recapitulate how this dance came to be, what the dance was, how performances were received, and how it felt to perform this work. I argue that the collaborative work introduced innovative techniques and elements that have since become part of the vocabulary and syntax of Navanritya or the New Indian Dance.[1]

These innovations were neither understood nor recognized by the dance community in 1984 when the work premiered in India; however, by 1993, the indigenous dance community was able to recognize clearly the same innovative elements.[2] In the intervening nine years, issues that had blocked perceptions of the work, such as notions of nationalism, reconstructed Indianness, and unacknowledged intercultural aesthetic hegemonies, had been confronted and successfully negotiated by more politically astute choreographers.

Dr Georg Lechner of the Max Mueller Bhavan had commissioned the original music by Igor Wakhevitch with my choreography.[3] The occasion was the first International East-

West Dance Encounter 1984, where choreographer dancers were invited to exchange views on their aesthetic endeavours with relationship to "East" (Indian classical dance tradition) and "West" (Euro-American theatre dance and modernity). Wakhevitch and I conceived and shaped the presentation together. Wakhevitch, a French citizen of Russian origin, trained by Olivier Messiaen and Pierre Schaffer, had been influenced by progressive rock music and had composed musical scores for Maurice Bejart and Carolyn Carlson. As with many New York-based dancers of my generation, I had studied Graham, Cunningham, and classical ballet techniques but had developed a dual cultural sensitivity enhanced by my involvement with Bharata Natyam and yoga. Wakhevitch and I discovered that we shared a mutual interest in yoga as it provides a system of modalities for working, both within and across our multicultural existences. During our joint presentation at the East-West Dance Encounter 1984, he said:

> I discovered immediately that between her and me, was the same approach of the

UTTARA ASHA COORLAWALA

life. We spoke the same language. What it is, this language? It is not a question of culture. I think it is the love of the universe. To feel really deep inside that not only are we a part of the universe, but we are the universe. And this universe can speak to us.... What will happen if suddenly this universe speaks to you with a little voice that you cannot tell it in words, but in your life it gives a lot of consequence. It gives to you immediately a new language.[4]

As the choreography developed, abstract ideas of time, space, and form transformed, appearing embodied as archetypal movers in the opening section "Postures". These movement images reappeared as motifs throughout the work. Here, I will focus on only two parts of the work, "The Birth of the Stars" and "Meditating" although the issues raised most vividly in their context pertain to the entire work.

"The Birth of the Stars"

"The Birth of the Stars" evokes archetypal concepts of creative time and space as female, and as envisioned in Shaivite texts. In doing so, the dance reflects back to us our proclivities at that time. Wakhevitch had been inspired by the dance vocables, thai-youm-da-thaa to elaborate repetitive minimalist versions of these sounds on his then new and innovative instrument, the electronic organ. The light whimsical repetitions of cascades of sound in his post-minimalist composition evoked a vivid image of the spontaneous self-generated play of the primordial Goddess (as) consciousness, expressed in the first sutra of the *Pratyabhijna-Hrydayam, Chitih svatantra*

vishvasiddhi hetuhu (Chiti creates the universe of Her own free will).

Chiti is supremely free. She is self-revealing.... She is Her own basis and support.... Desiring to create, She expands Herself of Her own free will. She manifests differences in Her being, appearing in countless forms and shapes. She becomes the five elements and combines them to make different life forms.... Creating all things She infuses them, becomes the universe, still She remains always exactly the same....[5]

"The Birth of the Stars" then became a dance of the hands involving the story-telling structures of the *padam*. We realized that small hand gestures might not be read in long or large spaces. This issue was addressed by extending the movements spatially. The wavelike undulations of the *pataka hasta* for water, for example, were augmented into undulating arm movements.

In modern dance abstraction, universalized experience and kinetic representations are valued, but in the classical Indian narrative forms, it is specificity, clarity, and multiplicity of details in narration that is valued. How then was the narrative in this dance to be so constructed as to be accessible as modern dance, and at the same time honour the cultural traditions that inspired its images?

The difficulty involved in honouring a culture-specific tradition of expression while still providing access paths to international audiences was recognized and acknowledged by New York dance critic Doris Diether, in her review:

Most accessible of the dancers was Uttara Coorlawala from India who performed two excerpts from her work "Winds of Shiva". Although based on a classical Indian dance with its emphasis on hand gestures, Coorlawala's "The Birth of the Stars" was joyful and lyric. Finger and hand gestures were cleanly articulated and, despite their smallness, were clearly visible. Dance patterns evolved from start to finish in a logical manner without breaks. Coorlawala moved effortlessly to the music composed and performed by Igor Wakhevitch.[6]

The dance begins as Shakti births. With vibrating *hamsasya hasta* she spins a web of sensual illusion from her belly.[7] Abstract scooping spiralling stirring wrist actions intermingle with the classical hand signs, juxtaposing the specific and abstract, the literal and symbolic.[8] Thus the classical hand signs are intermingled with natural and abstracted gestures and hand movements where the hands trace aerial patterns that correspond with the energy being "narrated". Jennifer Dunning described the same performance at New York University:

> The Indian choreographer smoothly blended a modern-dance attack and physicality with the *hastamudra* or hand gestures of Indian dance....
>
> Miss Coorlawala stretched and lunged, her hands curling through modified *mudra*s in a steady unspooling of dance....[9]

When executed with awareness, *asana* and the *hasta* are said to align the flow of *prana*. At the time when Rohinton Cama was helping me choreograph this dance, we did not know of specific connections between yogic practice and dance vocabulary. We knew that in several Indian cosmologies, the *panchabhuta*

(five elements), earth, water, fire, air, and ether/space are said to exist in the human body not only as physical constituents,[10] but also as subtle energy centres described in yoga as chakras.[11] One year later, after a performance in Nijmegen in the Netherlands (September 1985) I learned from Ad and Han Stemerding that the traditional hand gestures representing the elements in "The Birth of the

Stars" were in fact generating subtle energies corresponding to the elements characteristic of the chakras being represented! The Stemerdings, authorities in the Netherlands for their research in energy therapy, had been studying and experimenting with the use of hand gestures for energy therapy. It was Ad Stemerding who then suggested augmenting the subtle energies of the *hasta*s through correspondingly patterned body shapes.[12]

By offering mixed and multiple accessways to the work both in terms of movement techniques and also in terms of aesthetic, I contend that our collaborative choreography addressed postmodern concerns head on, even though this term had not gained currency at the time of choreographing and presenting this work.[13] Even as late as in 1993, a dance writer identified postmodern elements in another of my works but evaluated the work in terms of "fusion", a term that relates to the aesthetic criteria of modern dance.[14]

"Meditating"

"Meditating" is an improvised exploration of the movement characteristics of *asana* and *adavu* within and beyond their traditional frames of reference. The improvisations were guided by syntax characteristic of the *adavu* system, such as parallel symmetries of limbs, angular joint shapes, cycling arcs drawn by hands and feet with elbows and knees serving as radial centres for the arcs.[15] The *adavu* were slowed down and their shapes spatially augmented. Starting at an excruciatingly slow pace, the movements gradually transitioned from bound and formally articulated to flowing and shaping. The consistent slow pace was punctuated by occasional abrupt changes. Observant viewers noted that the sequence of *adavu* in the dance followed the traditional sequence in which *adavu* patterns are taught.[16] Hatha yoga *asana* (performed as *viniyoga* or flow sequences of postures) are interspersed with the manipulations of the *adavu*.

A sequence of computer images of a fifteen-dimensional star that evolves into simple or complex patterns is projected on to the backdrop. When "Meditating" begins, the dancer and the inner vision (here visualized as the *neelabindu* or the "blue pearl") are separate. As the dance proceeds, the dancer and the geometric images interact, echoing corresponding lines and angles. The patterns of light spread to cover the entire stage including the dancing body. The projections, side lights, and costumes combine to create a mysterious effect which, as one observer noted, seemed to dissolve boundaries between the dancing body and its environment.[17] While the timing of the projections structures the pace at which the dance develops, the geometrical sequence of the projections makes abundantly visible the Cartesian spatial dimensions of the *adavu* system. Finally, when the frame recedes, and the star shrinks till, at the end of the dance, it is found nestling on the dancer's forehead, its symbolism becomes obvious. The multi-faceted blue crystalline sphere stands for the *neelabindu*, the form of the casual body as seen in meditation. However, it is not symbolism, but the changing relationship between the dancer and the projections that generates the classic narrative of the journey from separation to unity.

Criteria for "correct performance" change according to the baggage of associations that each movement carries. This was one of the key issues I needed to confront as an intercultural performer. Is a consecutive linking of the *Mulabandha* and *Uddiyana Bandhas* (hatha yoga exercises to lock energy) the same as a "Graham contraction"? What transforms arabesque into *ardhachandrasana*, or conversely, is *ardhachandrasana* just a mis-performed arabesque? I began to play upon the relationships between similar movements in different languages such as the Graham technique, hatha yoga, Indian iconography, Bharata Natyam, classical ballet. With very slight changes in alignment and energy, movements could transition from one dance vocabulary to another.

Playing with minute changes of energy and shape is akin to the concept of *alap* in North Indian classical music. This formal

affinity was recognized at the opening performance by music lover Asha Sheth and by Sushilbhai Jhaveri, dance connoisseur and husband of the late Nayana Jhaveri, the eldest member of the Manipuri dance troupe of the Jhaveri Sisters. However, it seems not to have registered for the dancers and dance critics who read the movement as undifferentiatedly Western with sprinklings of Bharata Natyam. In 1986 Delhi dance critic Shanta Serbjeet Singh too saw the relationships: " 'Meditation' was indeed a deeply meditative piece, the nearest I have come to a danced 'alap' being played by a great master."[18]

Again, this was the first time an Indian audience was confronted with almost forty minutes of slow motion movement, and many did not seem to know what to make of it. However, *asana* and *adavu* in slow motion, spatial reconfigurations of familiar shapes, reappear in reminiscent but different configurations in Chandralekha's acclaimed work "Prana" in 1990. I contend that her presentations and vision educated audiences about indigenous movement traditions that had not been recognized in 1984. Consequently, when I showed excerpts from a 1985 videotaped performance of "Winds of Shiva" at the 1993 conference, dancers and critics who now could recognize the *asana* as indigenous to the Indian tradition, were surprised that they had not registered this aspect of the choreography.

Indologists and historians such as Kapila Vatsyayan and Romila Thapar attribute shared aesthetic qualities of some Eastern dance forms to common origins, in Sanskritic India,

5–7
In "Meditating", Uttara explored the specific connection between yogic practice and dance vocabulary and employed different yogasanas (postures) effectively. Photographs: Haresh Lalvani.

from where arts and mythologies travelled East along with the spread of Buddhism. Tracing the historical circulation of performance conventions is extremely complex, and made more so by current trends where dance practices are no longer geographically identifiable. Jennifer Dunning carefully observed that in a concert featuring four Asian choreographers, of Japanese, Chinese, Korean, and Indian origins, "a shared sense of concentration and focus distinguished the choreography and performing".[19] However, many French and American viewers attributed the pace of "Meditating" to the contemporary Japanese Butoh aesthetic whose slow-motion movement techniques and recent popularity among avant garde and new wave choreographers has undoubtedly influenced Western perceptions of manipulating time in dance. While *alap* involves slow audiovisual elaboration and playful exposition of the shifting relationships between microtones, there are profound philosophic and expressive differences between Butoh and the comparable Indian concepts. Butoh shares only the immediately apparent slowness of movement and condensed focus. The Butoh aesthetic of descent into the darker aspects of human nature, surprise, stylized nudity, and dangerous feats of physical risk find no correspondence in *alap*.

Who is Dancing? Performance as Reception

Improvising dance as meditation taught me to hold a simultaneous inner and outward focus. While mind, muscles, energies, and balancing mechanisms drew upon inner resources, performing elicited a kind of multi-focused awareness of distances and environments, of

faces, lights, surfaces, movements, and sounds both off and on stage. Images of sculptural postures, abstract impulses as inexplicable as a need to break into a run, to change path – these surfaced in my awareness simultaneously as my body performed them. Attuned, intoxicated with aliveness, my ears would see spaces, inner eyes directed my movements, soles of my feet listened, while I might observe a cockroach working its way across the cracks between the wooden planks of the stage floor.

Dancing, I could "know" changes in my environment, as light cues, as individual thoughts, from across the proscenium. It would seem as if the dance was disclosing its subtler dimensions and that these disclosures were somehow traceable to individuals in the audience as each dialogued silently with my activity. Like dream-messages from and to my body-mind, all of these sensations would change or inflect the set "choreography".

Choreography I learned could serve as juice (*rasa*), as flesh (dynamics and shapes), or as the skeleton (structure), or all three.[20]

Performing the same repertory often, showed me that dances have their own individual trajectories, now glowing with the soft luminescence of pearls, then twinkling like chandelier crystals, burning laser-precise paths, or churning relentlessly (*manthana*) like the ocean delivering up its gifts. Dancing intensified my sense of self. I learned that the experience of dancing is given, earned, and above all, shared. In the communion between dancer and audience, the dancer becomes a spectator. She watches the dance between her audience and the dance. So how should a performer receive reception?

8
Vrikshasana or tree pose from "Time". Photograph: Haresh Lalvani.

9
Alidha from "Heroism (Virya)". Photograph: Haresh Lalvani.

10
A pose from "Sensuality
(Shringara)". Photograph:
Haresh Lalvani.

Performance as Reception of Reception

I had revelled in the experiential dimensions
of creative action. Yet, at that time, I was not
prepared for the politically disastrous
consequences of acknowledging the same: that
to speak of the energy of a hand gesture can
be read as capitulation to Orientalistic visions
of Eastern mysteries; to speak of flow is to
turn into a New Age softhead; to speak of
love is to box oneself into hermeneutic mazes;
to express bhakti is to en-gender images of
weakness, of whining pining women, of sado-
masochistic fantasies of abject disciples and
controlling masters.[21]

In Europe, my work was celebrated for
fulfilling those characteristics that western
European audiences expect of Indian dance:
"transcendent" "sensual" "hypnotic"... rather
than as a contemporary statement. I
understand now by hindsight that I was
dancing in Ruth St Denis' shadow. Yet, as
often, and particularly then in East Germany

and the USSR, audiences (attuned to covert
signals perhaps?) brought intense focus to the
performances, attending as it were to the fine
print between the moves.

Radical Euro-American feminists read
intricate small gestures as "an external
decorative prettiness"[22] and danced allusions to
sculpture as being problematically embedded
with male constructions of femininity that
emphasize gender and seduction. Yet, other
American women celebrated the very same
dance for representing woman as
Progenitrix![23] A jury auditioning would-be
participants for a choreographer's workshop at
the Dance Theatre of Harlem, asked me
questions such as why I would show the icon
of Shiva in an otherwise abstract work. My
reply was that the icon is already an
abstraction in that it represents dense
philosophical concepts; could you abstract an
arabesque? Although colleagues had offered
responses, and authoritative figures had
pronounced judgement in the past, this
thoughtful jury had responded differently.
These eminent dancer personalities initiated a
dialogue.[24] Gradually, I began to appreciate the
meaning of performance as *darpana* (literally
mirror) or as reflection of the see-er's
proclivities.

Creativity, Difference, and Memory

India's historic monuments of worship and
dance invite the viewer to contemplate the
presence of creativity not as an individualistic
flow of talent and inspiration but rather as
anonymous service to a Higher Cause. Temple
sculptures generally were not autographed, not
marked by their makers. From my place in the
20th century, I envied our mytho-historical

artists free of the burden of having to be individually expressive; they could tap into the inner life of archetypal movements and images, without the anxiety that their representations might be old in the evanescent history of bodily representations. Despite years of involvement with modern dance and its history, rife with its myths of self-origination and individualism, I still speculate whether it is the abundance of historic representations of dance visible all over India that inflects my way of moving. Despite the futility of seeking assurances of primacy, I return to this question often, urged on by an unmistakable sense of bodily authenticity.

Looking outwards, my dancing body acknowledged, no, embraced, the imprints of colonial and intercultural discourses that many dancers and dance critics were denying in the India of this period of exclusively nationalist and Sanskritic reconstruction. Since the early '70s,[25] my dances acknowledged complex ambiguous contradictions, with juxtapositions and transitions between various movement vocabularies, disturbed notions about "East and West", the discreteness of authenticity, purity, and high art. Aesthetic boundaries marked by difference are devalued today, and internationalism is no heresy. Yet, in India, we continue to delve into our heritage, even as we recognize that its psycho-cultural meanings shift in response to changing paradigms. I have attempted a "thick" description here of some past performances as an insider distanced by temporal and geographic translocations. Having revisited past performances, I start to understand how writing casts a new written body on a past danced body. I re-member Winds....

NOTES

1. The Sanskrit term Navanritya (literally New Dance) was coined by Ranjabati Sircar with reference to her own choreographic approach but extended in an article by Simon Dove to include several choreographers working in India. See "Navanritya: New Frontiers of Indian Dance", *Sruti: Indian Classical Music and Dance Magazine* 75/76, December–January 1990.

2. Choreographers and dance critics at both the 1984 East-West Dance Encounter and the 1993 New Directions in Indian Dance event, both organized by Georg Lechner, included Andreine Bel, Chandralekha, Ileana Citaristi, Astad Deboo, Devisarro, Sunil Kothari, Susanne Linke, Sharon Lowen, Sonal Mansingh, Bharat Sharma, Daksha Sheth, Shanta Serbjeet Singh.

3. While I do not wish to discount the patriarchal circumstances around the initial production, Dr Lechner must be acknowledged for his profound concern with the state of Indian dance. His informed intuition brought together seemingly unlikely partners such as Daksha Sheth and Devisarro, Wakhevitch, Lalvani, and myself. The still ongoing connections initiated by Lechner resulted in much collaborative work particularly in the case of the Sheth-Devisarro team who have performed together since then, and continue to do so with their daughter Isha Sharvani. Unconcerned with local criticism, it was Lechner who first championed Chandralekha's radical vision. See comments by Pattabhi Raman in *Sruti* 200 (May 2002) in his article "No Room for Cultural Fascism in India's Multicultural Society" and in responses from readers in *Sruti* 202 (July 2002) and *Sruti* 203 (August 2002).

4. I am indebted to Max Mueller Bhavan and the National Centre for the Performing Arts for allowing me access to the audiotapes of the closed-door encounter sessions during this 1984 conference. During our joint presentation, Wakhevitch spoke as transcribed above.

5. Swami Muktananda Paramahamsa, *Commentaries on the Shiva Sutras and other Sacred Texts*, Oakland, California: SYDA Foundation, 1975, pp. 66–67.

6. Doris Diether, "An Array of Asian Dance at New York University Event", *The Villager*, New York, December 8, 1988.

7. In tantric practice the same *hasta* is called the *chinmudra* and is used as an energy "seal" to direct the flow of subtle energies in meditation.

8. "Throughout her work, Ms Coorlawala embellished standard dance vocabulary by deeply drawing from classical Indian forms and weaving them with Western dance idioms. The result was sophisticated and coherent. In her first excerpt, 'The Birth of a Star', [sic] elaborate hand gestures formed the foundation for movement that vacillated between the concrete and the abstract. Often her dancing was mimicry in nature. At one point her quickly quivering long slender fingers simultaneously suggested flight, a

rapid pulse or atomic emanations." J.L. Conklin, "Multimedia Effort at Peabody Displays Imagination, Craft", *The Baltimore Sun*, March 31, 1988.

9. Jennifer Dunning, "Asian Choreography in Two Sensibilities", *The New York Times*, December 6, 1988.

10. These correspondences are the basis of ayurvedic medical theory and practice.

11. The seven main energy centres are *muladhara* (earth) situated at the base of the spine; *swadhisthana* (water) located at the level of the sexual organs, *manipura* (fire) located above the diaphragm; *anahata* (air) at the heart level; *vishuddha* (ether) at the throat level; *ajna* (command) between the eyebrows; and the *sahasrara* (thousand-petalled lotus) in the crown of the head. There are several other energy centres whose locations and functions vary according to the different tantric systems, practices, and texts.

12. The Stemerdings' observations about the relationship between the *hasta* and the *chakra* were further corroborated in 1987 by the eminent dancer-scholar V.P. Dhananjayan who says that such correspondences are known to exist in the oral and written traditions of Bharata Natyam and Kathakali. Also T. Balasaraswati referred to a relationship between *hasta*(s) and subtle body energies in her Presidential Address at the 33rd annual conference of the Tamil Isai Sangam, Madras, December 21, 1975 reprinted in slightly different translations in both *Sruti* 5 (March 1984), p. 12, and in the *NCPA Quarterly Journal*, Vol XIII, No. 2, June 1984, pp. 78–79.

13. By postmodern dance, I refer to the aesthetics of postmodernism as described by Jameson and other scholars, rather than the term as used by Sally Banes to denote a chronological divide.

14. See Ananya Chatterjea, "The Throes of Change" in *The Economic Times*, New Delhi, March 28, 1993.

15. Kapila Vatsyayan has described movement characteristics of Bharata Natyam in her book *Classical Indian Dance* (Publications Division, New Delhi, 1974).

16. Among others I recall specifically that Matteo made this observation when he saw the dance in a studio in New York. Matteo is an exponent of traditional dance forms of Spain, India, and other countries in the anthropological and artistic tradition of La Meri.

17. Jack Anderson, "Peace Program at La Mama", *The New York Times*, March 18, 1986.

18. Shanta Serbjeet Singh, "Integrating Cultural Influences", *The Hindustan Times*, New Delhi, January 13, 1986.

19. See note 9.

20. See "Skin, Flesh and Bone" in Ze'ami's treatises as translated by Thomas Rimer and Yamazakin Masakazu in *On the Art of No Drama*, Princeton University Press, New Jersey, 1984, pp. 69–71.

21. See Carol Martin's argument regarding Sanjukta Panigrahi and Barba's intercultural theatre experiments in "The Body as Discourse" in *Women and Performance: A Journal of Feminist Theory*, Vol.

3, No. 2, #6, New York University, 1987–88.

22. Christine Temin, "Two Distinctive Forces Meet in One Program", *The Boston Globe*, January 20, 1988, writing of "The Birth of the Stars" at a performance at the Double Edge Theatre, Boston, as part of "Electra", a continuing project of women's international theatre.

23. Anne Rousseau, "Reflections on Festival '87, Sketches", *Sacred Dance Guild Journal*, Vol. 30, No. 1, Fall 1987.

24. Members of the panel included Arthur Mitchell, Bessie Schonburg, Mary Hinkson and others. I am still grateful to them all, especially Arthur Mitchell, for breaking the performer-as-object mode. I also acknowledge similar later discussions with Diane McIntyre, choreographer-griot.

25. See Robb Baker, "Liberated Dance: Out of the Concert Hall and into the Streets", *Dance Magazine*, 1970; Sunil Kothari, "A Fine Dance Recital", *Evening News of India*, August 21, 1973; Mithoo Coorlawala's article, "A Pioneer of Modern Dance in India", *AttenDance 2001*, cites various news articles and reviews including *The Times of India*, *Illustrated Weekly of India*, *Le Journal*, etc.

creating
endless possibilities

Astad Deboo

1

For many years I sought treasures
In faraway lands, across the seas in celestial
    palaces,
Hoping to become a very rich man
For many years I read the Holy Texts, and
    even Pascal,
Exchanged views with a sage on a hill-top
Hoping to become a very wise man
Until, one day I met a solitary old tree,
Who had grown wise
Accumulating treasures of leaves.

I was initiated into dance education at the age
of six in the steel town of Jamshedpur. An
age at which, although I was unaware of the
significance of the great dance tradition in
this country, like most precocious children, I
was interested in moving twinkle toes. In
dazzling my audiences of one and two.

In the mid-1960s I shifted to Mumbai. It
meant a cessation of dance, except for the
rare dance programme in college functions.
With a spirit of adolescent anguish, I was
confronted by a Murray Louis performance,
which was touring India. Louis' technique
and attention to physicality impressed me. It
questioned the basic foundations of dance

history. That performance was proposing a
theory called "decentralization".
Decentralization held that in depersonalizing
dancers through costume and design they
could be liberated from their own forms. For
Louis, this decentralization cut through the
very foundation of dance. Key to this idea
was the use of multimedia effects such as
experimental sound and projected light. Using
sound collage and changing images projected
onto both the stage and the dancers, the
choreographer could shift the focus away
from any one individual dancer, and
concentrate on the overall effect of the
production.

After the performance, I returned home
and stood before my favourite-most mirror,
and stretched my body like the American
dancers.

I relished this totally new form of dance
and movement, and when I tried it out at
home I found my body responded readily. I
knew what I wanted to do. I was bored out of
my mind doing economics – this was the new
direction I was looking for.

I was free.

Everyday, I devour my meal:
Of wheat and millet, along with organic
  plants and spices
Which praise the Earth
For generating invaluable fortunes
Which one day, I vow to return to Her.

The next two years were spent in introspection, and interrogation of the self. Thanks to Uttara Asha Coorlawala, I heard of Martha Graham and her ever-enveloping authority in the world of modern dance. For me, the legend of Martha Graham long ago became fact, just as her utterly personal technique has become part of the common vocabulary of dancers everywhere. "The centre of the stage is where I am," she once said. It still is.

I was at crossroads. Having studied Kathak under Guru Prahlad Das, from age eight to sixteen, I had to take that big leap. After contemplation and careful consideration, I resolved to simultaneously work with a multitude of forms, both Indian classical and modern dance.

After graduating from the University of Bombay, I travelled extensively across Europe to nurture "the seed of dance that was planted".

The summer of 1969, I hitchhiked my way to Europe. It was the wild '60s, and this was the thing to do. Adventure was planted in the head. I had to leave the shore. My game-plan was to use Europe as a springboard to America where I dreamt of taking classes in the Martha Graham technique. I dabbled in my share of idiocy. Ate a sumptuous meal in a restaurant and ran away without paying my bill, performed a thirty-minute show on Tehran TV for a bit of finance, at the drop-of-the-hat I would dance in people's homes, pubs, streets.

Herein I must digress and report an encounter I had with Sunil Shanbag's theatre group, Arpana in 1987. As Sunil Shanbag, theatre director and producer states:

There was talk about a possible collaborative performance with the musician, Brij Narain, the sarodist, with whom the group had done some work

2
Astad in a Kathakali pose.
Photograph courtesy
Astad Deboo.

earlier. Like most classical musicians, Brij was cautious. He'd only heard of Astad's work in an oblique way. A meeting was arranged at Brij's home.

Once there, Astad asked for a recording of Brij Narain's music. An audiocassette was produced. It was a scratchy recording of a concert, but as soon as Astad heard the first notes, he went into a crouch and began to respond intuitively. The small room was cramped with furniture, and Astad tried to transform it into a performance space. Every inch of available space was used, with whirling arms and legs. A dhurie lying rolled up in a corner became a prop, an extension of the body, a straight-backed chair added unusual angles as it stood on one leg, and a door opened and closed in counterpoint to the rhythm of the tabla.

At the end of this little demo the sarod maestro stood up and embraced Astad. He said: "This is the room where I teach my students. I use it every day. But today it is as though I am seeing it for the first time."

I did a collaborative performance with Sunil Shanbag's actors, who were not trained dancers. There was an open-air show at the Elephanta Dance Festival, Mumbai. Such incandescence of space was possible with dance techniques.

This was the similarity with my hitchhiking. I tried to cross borders, jump over boundaries, and not be bogged down. I exchanged tips with fellow back-packers, gatecrashed into museums, interacted with locals and understood the idiosyncrasy of towns, districts. My thumb-rule was simple: the journey had to be fascinating.

Once in England, my plans collapsed, since a visa to the USA was not forthcoming. And so I began travelling extensively, taking classes where I could, and investing considerable time in Japan, where I got a close look at the traditional dance theatres of Kabuki. I allowed myself to be lowered from a tall crane into vats of colour and then onto a large white cloth on which I danced-out a painting!

My first long exposure to the wider world of dance and art happenings was heady. When I returned to India, I was eager. For most in the audience, the idea of dance was new, and so I used straightforward narratives. I tried to create sparse and beautiful designs. I replaced flat backdrops with three-dimensional objects. I tried to contribute to the art of stage design and dance production. But ultimately I was hoping for a continued experimentation, by focusing my constant attention to human emotion, frailty, and perseverance. This was a running theme in my early work. In "Ritual", I was lowered into a circle of burning candles, and I proceeded to drip molten wax onto my body. In "Asylum", I was a schizophrenic who sucked on his big toe imagining it was my baby. In "Broken Pane", I stuck a syringe into my arm and then pounded my forehead on the stage floor in a drug-induced frenzy. The depiction of emotion was very raw...bloody.

I feel the present representation of classical Indian is over-concerned with flow and grace. It has forgotten the more violent traditional passions. I felt, through the spastic movements, tremblings, and falls I could express emotional and spiritual themes ignored by other dance. I desired to evoke strong emotions, and achieved these visceral responses through the repetition of explicitly, violently disjunctive movements.

Maybe this world is another planet's hell.

And then, away from the murky, gloomy world we inhabit, there is this yearning, someplace-somewhere to slip into quietness. That is, much-more measured, deliberate and non-figurative. Keep stretching the horizon, a little further, every time.

Even today, dance remains a driving passion and in spite of all the pitfalls one is constantly attempting to grow.

3

I had no place I could call my home
I was a citizen of the world
I had no address
I was a visitor on this planet
And I was merely passing through
In the hope that I would befriend
    someone, anyone
On this trip.

I hitchhiked my way across Europe. When I returned to India in 1972, I studied Kathakali under Guru E.K. Pannicker. This was followed by "sell-out" shows the world-over at major international dance festivals which included the notable choreography of Maia Plisseskaia;

3
Astad Deboo and Dadi Pudumjee in "Thanatamorphia". Photograph: Mahendra Sinh.

4
Astad in "Basics". Photograph: Farrokh Chothia.

5 (*opposite*)
Astad in "Passage of Life". Photograph: Farrokh Chothia.

ASTAD DEBOO

performances with Pink Floyd; and collaborations with Ratan J. Batliboi, Suresh Bhojwani, Satyadev Dubey, Sunil Shanbag, Dadi Pudumjee, Pong Chalam Drummers of Manipur along with performances, workshops, lectures all of which has added to my body of work.

Through the Max Mueller Bhavan in Mumbai, I was introduced to Pina Bausch. She saw me perform. On cue, I was at the Wuppertal Dance Company, Germany. It's difficult to think of another European dance artist who has continued throughout her career to be both as influential and as controversial as the German choreographer Pina Bausch. Her sensibility is firmly European in the visions of a dark, brooding, and tension-filled world her theatre depicts. It is said, long before the British sculptor Damien Hirst was displaying butchered animals preserved in formaldehyde, Bausch was pioneering something close to the dance equivalent, the body under physical and emotional assault suspended in time and space by the framing device of the stage. Physically, Bausch's dances are highly visual and textural, as much as spectacles, and this adds to their visceral impact.

For me those few weeks were high on kinetic energy, but it didn't work out. Basically, there were two problems. She wanted to base some of her work on loose borrowings from Kathakali. I was resolute that I wouldn't do such a thing. My argument being, that although I'm Indian, I'll add my little flourishes and gestures. She didn't like it. She said: "You can stay and observe but you're not part of the team."

This meant another uprooting for me. This has been my modus operandi. Whenever a situation gets comfortable, I reject it, and hurl myself with renewed verve and vitality into a new one.

Always, an uncertain tomorrow... everything is very tenuous.

I'm weary of prosceniums. Of the traditional stage which reduces all formations to frontal viewing. I tried to unshackle myself from the narrow walls of domesticity. Which is why I've always been open to performing site-specific works. Be it Champaner, Chandigarh, or a Chettinad home in Chennai. And even the

famous dance performance on The Great Wall of China. That was simple. A friend and I had a portable music system, a few props, and my costume. We would walk. Identify a performance-site. Ready ourselves and perform. This went on for a few hours. The audiences were receptive and the feedback was super.

The point is, in my work of dance, I use totally new forms or at best take parts of our existing vocabulary of Indian classical dance and combine them with other forms. Such a thing is viewed with scepticism. Although, herein, it is interesting to note that when I began my work I did very story-like narratives. That way I created an audience. Much later, I grew bolder. I introduced the "abstract" element and experimented with music, with puppets, with themes.

In my work at the National Gallery of Modern Art, Mumbai, "Five Minus Three (Audience on Two Levels)", I used the over-elaborate space and got the audience to follow the performance. Horizontally and vertically. There were other worthy-of-note performances at the St Xavier's College quadrangle, CST Railway Station, and a whole assortment of festivals in Norway, Brazil, France. Similarly, I presented a sketch in the mid-'80s for which Ratan J. Batliboi designed a box with open slots. Due to this, the whole was never visible. Just fragmented viewing. A wrist, an ankle, the chest. It was a constant shift between the seen and unseen. Rajani and Tamas. It was an attempt at questioning distortions in perspective.

What you see is not necessarily what you get.

Later, I experimented with abstract geometric forms and spare structures, my works like "Zontas" (about an astronaut going into space) and "Thanatomorphia" can stun with their fusion of strict form and deep emotion. Simplicity masks complexity. In times such as ours, it is difficult to create a work, which is delicate, immaculate. Obviously, such an endeavour has untold risks. Inadvertently there's the intrusion of unevenness, of flashiness. One tries to be quiet, introspective, inward looking, and meditative.

When an artist is able to share that quality with the audience, it is dreamlike.

4

What the prudent old man told me in
  my sleep!
Remember: The tranquillity which
  surrounded Beethoven's head
Was not the end
It was the beginning of music.

Aldous Huxley has said: After silence that which comes nearest to expressing the inexpressible is music.

For me, what Huxley says is true. I've always been attracted to the sound of things. I've diligently attended music concerts from Hindustani classical to opera, from new age to street musicians. I'm a big collector of music. I've friends all over the world who have been kind and supportive. A music composer in Berlin runs an alternative music store. This gives me the opportunity to partake of all kinds of world music.

Just as dance can be made of everyday gestures, music can be minimal. With me, music has been everything. The centre of attraction, sometimes supplementary, sometimes silence.

Here I must mention my collaboration (and friendship) with the Gundecha Brothers, who are the purest exponents of Dhrupad *gayaki* today. Until then, Hindustani classical was never an integral part of my conceptualization. That was because I had

neither context nor reference point. Furthermore, I was not keen to use it merely because the sitar or the tabla was the in thing. I found the *alap*s too long; and the traditionalists were mortified whenever I chopped off bits.

Then I heard a recital by the Gundecha Brothers in Bhopal. I was very moved. I made my introduction, and broached the possibility of working together. They were still with their Guru. So we did a work-session on a trial, as a work-in-progress kind of thing. You must bear in mind that the Gundecha Brothers had not confronted my type of dance and movement earlier.

Soon enough, I was invited to perform at the Khajuraho Dance Festival. On Satyadev Dubey's advice, I performed Muktibodh's "Lakdi ka Ravan". I had stanzas from the poem read out. The Gundecha Brothers sang. And I danced. It was a genuine collaboration.

I made a theatrical entry. This was post Rajiv Gandhi. So we had a *lal-batti wallah* official car. My backstage team was converted into Black Cats with their AK-47s. I strutted with the customary fanfare one associates with a *mantri*. On stage, I oozed self-importance and vanity, even as I methodically started disrobing an assortment of garments, which symbolized the tiers in our society.

And there were others.

I worked in England at King Alfred's College in Winchester with music composer Francis Silkstone who composed music for the myth of Orpheus and Eurydice. In this piece, "Trying Orpheus", Orpheus is on trial after he has lost Eurydice in the underworld. The dance was accompanied by the singing of Amelia Cuni, an Italian singer, who trained in the Dhrupad School under the Malliks. Then there was the Brazilian singer Louis Gonzagiana Jr, who later died in a car crash. He sang, I danced.

And there were others.

Percussionists from Africa, Europe, Cuba, Brazil. I have jammed with Peter Hammel, Germany for the Festival of Vienna. This was under the directorship of Reinhart Flatischer. I treasure the work with the Indian virtuosos, Shubha Mudgal, Uday Bhavalkar, Zakir Hussain, Sivamani, Louis Banks. In China, I closed my act with a piece of bravado. This would be an improvised piece wherein I would perform with a Chinese musician. It could be a classical or folk musician; a singer or instrumentalist. I took the plunge into the unknown, with the "unknown" musician. The audience were flabbergasted. More so, when they realized that the piece was totally unrehearsed. At times, I met the musician for the first time on the stage, in front of the audience. The whole experience was luminous.

It was trouble-free. I followed a simple axiom: Remember, the wise man makes more opportunities than he finds.

5

Every time my friends ask me for the
road into the sea
I show them a path
But they don't see it.
Maybe they don't want to...
Or maybe they cannot sense the
goodness of the waves
From the distant shore.

For two decades I've worked as a solo performer. I still perform solo works but there came a time when I felt that the Indian performing scenario was a little more amenable and receptive to group works. I collaborated with Dadi Pudumjee and his Puppets, and later, the Gundecha Brothers. I've always been an ardent supporter of the performing arts. I'd seen the Thang-ta martial art form twenty years ago. But I was keenly aware that such a work would need resources and a stretch of time. I was commissioned for a project and they wanted something different. Since I had a

working idea, I travelled to Imphal and met Guru Devabrata Singh, who is the guru of the Hula Group. I sought his permission.

I was mesmerized by the form of the Hula and their Thang-ta (sword-spear) technique. In implicit manner, I could relate it to my form and me. They were open to trial and tests. While collaborating and working with my four Hula co-dancers, I've always bounced-off ideas and used their technique. Adding a bit of mine, use their basic idiom.

The work has grown. Now, it is "Celebrations".

7
Astad Deboo and the martial art performers of Imphal in "Celebrations". Photograph: Farrokh Chothia.

ASTAD DEBOO

My interest in working with challenged communities led to my work with the Calcutta-based Action Players, a group of hearing-impaired theatre-actors. My first encounter with them is fresh in my memory. They were a group of talented actors silently resolved on taking up the challenge of dance. I've worked and workshopped with them. These sessions attempted to focus attention on synchronization, familiarizing with different spaces, and mirror exercises for reflexes. The Action Players (like the deaf groups I worked with in Mexico and Hong Kong) had to approach these sessions with a deep sense of commitment and respect. This was a theatre group of non-dancers that had to be moulded into nimble and snazzy dancers. The arduous journey had begun.

Because of my work with the Action Players, I was invited by Gallaudet University, USA (which is perhaps the world's first university for the deaf), with the aim of expanding the scope of the work and exploring the possibility of bringing the hearing-impaired communities of both countries together in a festive atmosphere of sharing.

A breakthrough was achieved during the Young Scholar's Programme in Washington. The subject was: India. So I did a basic expose of Indian dance theatre, field trips in Washington wherein they visited a Hindu temple; a puja exhibition at the Smithsonian; called on an Indian home where the hostess organized a fashion show. I invited Indian dancers who lived in the DC area to demonstrate. In the second phase, the Americans travelled to India and performed and workshopped. In the third phase, the Action Players, 21 in all, travelled to the USA. The idea was that hearing-impaired students from manifold cultures come together and push the boundaries of expression farther and farther.

This was a real exchange of dance techniques, and the workability of ideas.

In my first work with the Action Players, "The Dancing Dolphins", we explored basic concepts such as space, the possibilities of the body, and physical synchronization. I was able to tap into the resources of the Action Players for an extended period. They began to internalize dance, and in their exploration of abstract movement and rhythm they communicated with each other as dancers. This was done through an elaborate pattern of counts.

In "Circle of Feelings", they travelled that extra distance due to the intense group work. A journey had begun.

In this sense, I was extremely pleased about the invitation to the international festival, "Deaf Way II" in Washington. To start with, more than eight thousand hearing-impaired would attend the festival. The event had attracted more than two thousand entries of which only 25 were selected and our group was one of them.

Somewhere, by performing both in India and abroad, I've been trying to ensure that the notion "there's no such thing as an ideal dance structure" be accepted. I've tried to make my audiences aware of the physical apparatus and how much dance can do to make the body more mobile, flexible, expressive, even sensitive, among the hearing-impaired in India, China, Mexico, the USA.

I've also come into association with the dancers at Clark School for the Deaf in Chennai. My interaction with R. Karthika, who was the best classical dancer in the Chennai group, has only now begun. Her talent and rigorous training in Bharata Natyam, gives her

the resources both to be inventively collaborative, and rooted, at the same time.

Today, I hope "First Step" is just that...a first step in a series of such encounters.

A newer creation. An improved array of ideas. Extra melancholic, extra humane.

As that infamous absurdist playwright said: The future is not what it used to be! Quite true, the possibilities are endless.

6

Since

The man

With the calliper

Could not enter the

Sea

And swirl along with

Waves

He sat on the shore

And dreamt about make-believe

Creatures

Who whirled out of the foam

In the dark of night.

NOTE
I am grateful to Ramu Ramanathan, who has helped put my thoughts into words, and specifically composed the six shorts in appreciation of my body of work.

Extensions at Home and Abroad

dance
in films

Arundhathi Subramaniam

We may wince at its incongruities, scoff at its sense of overblown fantasy, roll our eyes heavenward at its bump-and-grind antics. But the fact remains that Indian film dance is an organic and integral part of our collective consciousness.

And although like popular art forms, it is intended to reflect contemporary social values – including the vulgar, the superficial, and the ephemeral – it is truly amazing how many film dances remain enshrined in our cultural memories.

Who can forget Helen's provocative-but-never-crass cabaret, "*Aa jaane jaan*", in *Inteqam*? Or Rekha's body language of subtle subtext as the celebrated courtesan in the "*In aankhon ki masti se*" number in *Umrao Jaan*? Or the flamboyant jugalbandi between Vyjayanthimala and Helen in *Prince*? Or Waheeda Rehman's lyrical grace in the "*Kaanton se kheenchke ye aanchal*" paean to freedom in *Guide*? Or even Hema Malini's legendary dance on glass smithereens in *Sholay*? One suspects that the mind-boggling boneless fluidity of Prabhudeva in "*Muqabla*", Madhuri Dixit's vibrant sensuality in "*Ek, do, teen*", Shahrukh Khan's spirited "*Chhaiyya chhaiyya*" routine on the moving train, or

Aishwarya Rai's ethereal *dandiya* number, "*Dhol baaje*", could well be counted among the golden moments of Hindi film dance in the future.

Strangely, despite its unabashedly hybrid identity that has perennially revelled in cultural "contaminations" of all kinds, the rhetoric of "purity" continues to pervade popular film criticism. We continue to speak of an age when dance was cleaner, less vulgar, more original, less Westernized, less manic, less robotic – always forgetting that "antiquity", as Voltaire reminded us long ago, "is always full of eulogies of another more remote antiquity". Nostalgia, as always, is a great fictionalizer.

Thus, dance in Hindi cinema – like cinema itself – has had a colourful, messy, variegated, non-linear history, its journey shaped by chaotic cocktails of capricious markets, serendipitous encounters, idiosyncratic forgeries and re-appropriations, individual talents and tastes. The absence of any comprehensive documentation on the subject doesn't make the matter any easier for anyone who chooses to investigate the area. Trends, therefore, are difficult to map, and

1

Sadhana Bose as a court dancer in Madhu Bose's film *Raj Nartaki* (produced in Hindi, Bengali, and English in the year 1941). The dances were not specifically based on any known classical dance forms, but were inspired by the Manipuri dance tradition. Photograph courtesy National Film Archive of India, Pune.

new directions only fuzzily discernible. Nonetheless, it would be impossible to discuss even the potential journeys and embryonic impulses – however protean the scene might be – without some sense of the changing context down the decades.

Firstly, it is clear that the song-and-dance number is an integral part of Indian cinema that cannot be wished away. As film historian Rosie Thomas elucidates, Western critics and the Indian middle-class intelligentsia have long tended to evaluate Indian cinema "according to the canons of European and Hollywood film-making" and "film-making practices that it has itself rejected". To wonder why Indian cinema cannot aspire to the realism of a Western cinematic aesthetic, as many do, is, then, to miss the point.

For the forces that have shaped the identity and destiny of Indian cinema have been culturally and historically specific. While Indian cinema has been chromosomally linked to the market since its very inception, the artistic influences range from performance traditions of *nautanki*, *jatra,* and Parsi theatre (which in itself is a melange of Indian folk idioms and European theatre techniques) to classical Sanskrit aesthetics, as scholar Amit Rai points out. Evidence of the latter is clearly available in the varied stylistic characteristics intrinsic to Indian cinema: the presence of the three "Akademis": Sangeet Natak, Lalit Kala, and Sahitya, the non-linear itemized narrative with its interludes of comedy, fights, music-and-dance (wherein the story is itself one component among others), even the culinary metaphor common to both (for the masala movies obviously aspire to achieve the right blend of flavours in order to evoke *rasa*).

Conventionally, the history of dance in Indian film is traced to the advent of the talkies in 1931. However, scholar V.A.K. Ranga Rao cites the instance of "music-dictated movement" in a film as far back as Dadasaheb Phalke's *Lankadahna* (1917), which suggests that the ingredient was by no means a stranger to the silent era either.

However, it was when cinema acquired a "voice" that the issues of language and

regional particularity became fraught. Hindi cinema (which constituted twenty per cent of the total production) now stepped in to play the vital role of a pan-Indian cinema – a function conferred upon it by an increasingly patriotic zeitgeist that sought to construct a homogeneous unifying national identity. The capacity of the song-and-dance number to transcend cultural and linguistic barriers became yet another factor behind its ubiquity at the time, and, no doubt, remains an important reason to this very day.

By the mid-1940s, playback singers had already arrived on the scene, and actors were no longer required to possess musical skills. However the growing vigour and pace of the dance sequences clearly necessitated that actors hone their dancing skills considerably. Movements grew more stylistically varied, crafted, and demanding, as dance choreography began to emerge as an important independent sphere in the movie-making process.

Gradually, over the decades the slow-paced languorous solo and duet were replaced increasingly by adrenaline-infused numbers – usually large ensemble pieces. Particularly with the surge of action-oriented cinema from the mid-'70s onwards, the mandatory *vilambit* lovelorn number was increasingly relegated to the background and every second or third song was, and continues to be, accompanied by fast-paced dances. Additionally, the willing suspension of disbelief – always a vital requisite in Indian cinema – was liberally extended to allow lovers in rural India to carouse along the snow-kissed Alps and breakdance furiously along the sun-drenched beaches of Mauritius, before returning to their respective realities – all in the course of a single song.

A significant characteristic of Hindi film dance (discussed by anthropologist Peter Manuel in the context of its music) is its

2
A sequence from *Raj Nartaki*, where Sadhana Bose as gopi offers water to Lord Krishna. The backdrop, costumes, and idols of Krishna and Radha on a swing are inspired by Manipuri Rasalila with some variations. Photograph courtesy National Film Archive of India, Pune.

ARUNDHATHI SUBRAMANIAM

Closely allied to its hybrid and syncretic nature, however, is also the standardization of the song-and-dance sequence – a long-term feature of Indian cinema. Thus the "folk dance" in Hindi cinema is, almost by definition, "exotic" and "folksy" because regional features have to be ironed out to make it seem like it could be performed in almost any hamlet in the country. The essentialized "jhatak-matak" style, for instance, is now considered to epitomize the sexy gait of the archetypal Indian village damsel from Rampur to Rameshwaram – and

3 and 4
S.S. Vasan produced *Chandralekha* in Tamil and Hindi in 1948 and introduced spectacular dance sequences. In these two illustrations the dancers are seen performing on the drums, creating fascinating visuals. The dances and the decorative costumes drew inspiration from Bharata Natyam. Photographs courtesy National Film Archive of India, Pune.

artistic syncretism – an ability to appropriate elements of diverse vocabularies and integrate them into a quintessential film dance chutney. The result of such unabashed borrowing is rarely a heap of quotations, however; indeed, the end-product is only deemed successful if it creatively integrates and transforms these elements into something that works within the parameters of cinematic and box-office acceptability.

may well have been re-appropriated today by various folk dance traditions as well! (In fact, to what extent the homogenized Hindi film folk dance has, in turn, influenced folk dance practitioners would be an interesting subject for a research study. Has its market-driven aesthetic had an alienating effect, or has it merely been creatively internalized by forms that have, in any case, always transacted artistically with other folk idioms?)

Creative loans from folk and classical dance idioms were common in Hindi cinema early in the day. The aesthetic influence of choreographers like Gopi Krishna and more obliquely, Uday Shankar and those who trained under him, surely shaped the approach to dance in film in the '50s. The emergence of heroines trained in classical dance, such as Vyjayanthimala, Waheeda Rehman, Asha Parekh, and Padmini, among others, also gave fillip to this choreographic strain.

It is often believed that Western movement vocabularies permeated Indian cinema only in the post-Independence era. However, V.A.K. Ranga Rao points to various instances (such as the dances in Madhu Bose's film *Court Dancer* in 1941, for example) of the impact of Hollywood on Indian film dance in the '30s and '40s. Nonetheless, it was in the '50s and '60s that the overt influences of the waltz, rumba, samba, jive, rock 'n' roll, shake, twist, and cha-cha-cha began to be apparent

in Hindi cinema. The panache and cheerful eclecticism that characterized the dances of Bhagwan, for instance, influenced several after him, including dance directors like Krishna Kumar, Surya Kumar, and P.L. Raj who perpetuated his approach with their own individual permutations.

The rise of the action film in the late '70s and '80s and the increasing exposure of the Indian middle class to Western popular dance and music heralded the flamboyant advent of rock and disco. With the revival of the musical family-oriented romance film (such as *Qayamat Se Qayamat Tak* in 1988, *Chandni* and *Maine Pyaar Kiya* in 1989, *Hum Aapke Hain Kaun* in 1994, *Dilwale Dulhaniya Le Jayenge* in 1995, and *Kuch Kuch Hota Hai* in 1998), dance in Hindi cinema has clearly grown slicker, more glamorous, and youth-oriented, reflective of an affluent consumerist post-liberalization Indian lifestyle. The upsurge of bhangra-pop, dandiya-jazz, disco-kathak,

6 and 7
Front and back covers of the booklet for Uday Shankar's film *Kalpana* (1948), a disguised biography of the legendary dancer with several dances choreographed by him, the only record of his creations. The aesthetics of this film shaped the approach to dance in the films of the 1950s. Photographs courtesy Sunil Kothari dance collection.

even kalari-breakdance syntheses also epitomize an ethos of conscious cultural hybridization. The growth of the Indian middle class in an era of globalization, the boom in international communication networks, and the growing markets in the diaspora are, no doubt, responsible for these changes – many of which are evident in Yash Chopra's *Dil To Paagal Hai* (1997), for instance, where the dance routines seem to be set in quasi-New York style apartments and dance studios, and clearly attempt to recreate the modern bourgeois urban aesthetic of the Indian young and privileged.

Today there are, on an average, six to eight songs in a Hindi film, several of which are accompanied by frenzied dance routines. (*Hum Aapke Hain Kaun*, a runaway success, boasted of fourteen songs, almost all of which were accompanied by dance sequences.) Many lament the growing disjunction between the song-and-dance sequence and the film plot. Director Raj Kapoor is quoted as having said that if you missed a single song in his film, you missed an important link between one part of the narration and the next. Few directors would make that claim today.

However, while this is one function of the song-and-dance, it is clearly not the only one; for it is often intended to actively interrupt the narrative, rather than segue seamlessly into it. With the impact of television and MTV in particular, the relative autonomy of this sequence has increased, and the music-and-dance video is now launched well in advance of the film itself.

Moreover, song-and-dance has frequently been an aesthetic device to transport film lovers and viewers into a dreamspace, undefined by socio-economic realities and heedless of the unities of time and place. It is possible here for a middle-class small-town heroine to metamorphose into a jiving, disco-savvy, skimpily attired cosmopolitan young woman. It is equally possible here for the young NRI heroine to transform into a wide-eyed "village lass", performing a folk dance in the idyllic mustard fields of Panjab, with the fluid ease of a seasoned daughter of the soil.

8
A Manipuri dance sequence from *Kalpana*. Photograph courtesy Amala Shankar.

A significant related phenomenon in recent times has been the gradual disappearance of the vamp-and-cabaret-artiste. It was a role that dancers like the legendary Helen – a magnificent dancer who elevated the near-farcical gyrations demanded of her species into uninhibited and free-flowing dance sequences that never seem to age – performed from the '50s, through the '60s right until the '70s.

However, the dichotomy between the chaste heroine (who could only perform the

over-optimistic thesis. For even while the heroine is permitted a certain measure of sartorial variety and freedom of movement – she can zigzag between miniskirts and ghagras, Kathak chakkars and jazz, with enviable fluency – she still remains confined within the *Lakshman rekha* of a hero-oriented, neo-feudal cinema. Glamour doll or "Bharatiya naari", she continues to lack agency and volition; her lot, even as she capers and prances with Dionysian abandon, is to wait for her *dilwala* to come and claim her as his *dulhaniya*.

The impact of the MTV dance video on Hindi cinema of the '90s has been much discussed in the media. Evidence of this is discernible in the emphasis on sleek and glossy dance sequences, fast cuts, special effects, hip designer apparel, slimmer bodies in the chorus lines, and of course, the choreography. Interestingly, dance choreographers like Saroj Khan, Farah Khan,

9
V. Shantaram's *Jhanak Jhanak Payal Baje* (1955) showcased classical Kathak dances with the Kathak exponent Gopi Krishna who choreographed several numbers, dancing with the actress Sandhya. Shiva and Parvati are seen on Mount Kailas with Ganapati and Nandi bowing before them. Photograph courtesy National Film Archive of India, Pune.

garba in the village square) and the Westernized "scarlet woman" (whose role was to perform a seductive cigarette-and-wineglass-wielding belly-dance in a smoky bordello) has obviously faded today. It is tempting to view the exultant spontaneous dance numbers of Urmila Matondkar in *Rangeela* as the coming-of-age of the Indian heroine. However, this seems like a somewhat

10
A song and dance sequence from *Hum Aapke Hain Kaun* (1994) with Madhuri Dixit (centre). Photograph courtesy National Film Archive of India, Pune.

139

11 and 12

The arrival of Saroj Khan, aka Masterji as dance choreographer in Hindi films marked an important moment in the development of film dance. With her understanding of the medium and her approach to training, she has carved a niche for herself. Photographer Dayanita Singh has effectively captured the mood of rehearsals on the sets. Here, Saroj Khan directs Rekha in *Kismat ki Rekha* where in one song Rekha goes through six personas, including finally that of a Thai princess! Photographs: Dayanita Singh.

Arundhathi Subramaniam

13
Saroj Khan directing Madhuri
Dixit on the sets of *Prem
Granth*. Photograph: Dayanita
Singh.

14
Saroj Khan directing a group
dance number on the sets of
Prem Granth. Photograph:
Dayanita Singh.

and Shiamak Davar are familiar names to the general audiences today. Frequently interviewed by the press and television, their names featuring prominently on film promos, they have acquired celebrity status – something that would have been unthinkable in the past when only music composers, in addition to the director, were considered worthy of mention. The fact that it is kosher for the hero (Anil Kapoor) in *Taal* to play a dance choreograper is also proof, as sociologist Rahul Srivastava highlights, of how glamorous dance in Hindi cinema has become. (Even the character played by Shahrukh Khan in *Dil To Paagal Hai* seems to be essentially a dance choreographer, although he is ostensibly a theatre director.)

Moreover, when someone such as Shiamak Davar (who trained at the Pineapple School of Dance in New York and runs hugely popular jazz ballet classes in Mumbai) is invited to choreograph dance in mainstream movies like *Dil To Paagal Hai* and *Taal* – which also happen to be huge box-office successes – it only confirms that the new chapter in Hindi film dance has, indeed, opened. Davar himself believes that what differentiates him from his precursors is his emphasis on "precision, coordination, and above all, fit and agile bodies" (since his dancers happen to be trained professionals).

Not surprisingly, there are many who fear

15 and 16
A dance sequence choreographed by Vaibhavi Merchant for *Mumbai se Aaya Mera Dost* (2003).
Photographs: John Panikar.

ARUNDHATHI SUBRAMANIAM

that dance in Hindi cinema since the '90s runs the danger of losing its identity under the onslaught of Western cultural standardization. Yesteryear filmstar and dancer, Vyjayanthimala, rues that the camera "does all the dancing" nowadays, while veteran dance choreographer P.L. Raj describes the contemporary film dance scene as "PT drill" and dance icon, Helen, dismisses it as mere "gymnastics". Even the current rage, Shiamak Davar, seems to feel that "the element of performance" is growing progressively scarcer in film dance.

While the premium on pace and jazz-inspired routines is undeniable, it is equally indisputable that the impact of the West has been evident in Indian cinema ever since its inception, as discussed earlier. Moreover, it is interesting to read a writer in a 1966 issue of *Filmfare* bemoaning the "crude callisthenics" that masquerade as film dance. Ironically, many would today consider the dances of the '60s as representative of a more refined and gracious era.

On closer examination, then, it is clear that the element of pastiche, always an integral feature of Indian cinema, is still alive and well. Hindi cinema, as scholar Anil Saari puts it, has always been "an eclectic, assimilative, imitative and plagiaristic creature that is constantly rebelling against its influences.... Everything that it borrows from the Euro-American scene, it distorts and caricatures." Even the nostalgia for the songs

and dances of the past that seem to recall a simpler world, has been tapped by several hit films of the present, suggesting that terms like "cultural imperialism" are facile and inadequate formulations to describe the state of dance in cinema today.

The celebration of the "folksy" aesthetic in Sanjay Leela Bhansali's *Hum Dil De Chuke Sanam*, and the triumph of old Himachal folk songs and dances in an international competition in Subhash Ghai's *Taal*, suggest that dance in Hindi cinema is by no means asphyxiated by a globalized mass culture. And surely it is not a mere coincidence that the dancer-heroine (Madhuri Dixit), who is equally adept at Kathak and jazz, hooks the hero in Yash Chopra's *Dil To Paagal Hai*, thereby triumphing romantically over the other dancer (Karisma Kapoor) whose body seems entirely conditioned by Western dance vocabularies?

Moreover, while watching what is supposedly an Italian folk dance in *Hum Dil De Chuke Sanam*, the hero's memory nostalgically transports him to the folk dances back home. What makes this counterpoint interesting is the fact that it seems to acknowledge the rich folk traditions of two cultures, rather than a trite juxtaposition of "ancient" Indian culture with the artistically and morally "dissolute modernism" of the West — a frequent trope in Hindi cinema.

In the hit film, *Humse Hai Muqabla* (the dubbed Hindi version of the Tamil film, *Kaadalan*, 1994), the hero, Prabhudeva, with his extraordinarily versatile body, engages in a deliberate movement pastiche of a maelstrom of contemporary cultural influences. We see all the images of a fast-mutating world, and yet we also see the ability of a cinema to

withstand, even co-opt potentially hegemonic forces – to borrow, but on its own terms. In an article for the *Journal of Arts and Ideas*, Vivek Dhareshwar and Tejaswini Niranjana point out that in the famous "Peta rap" song-and-dance sequence, the hero's intrusion into the upper caste/class heroine's Bharata Natyam dance school with his zany and inimitable mix of rap and folk, also becomes an indictment of the history of Indian classical dance – the appropriation of a lower caste dance form like sadir by the middle-class brahman elite. They

17
Helen in one of her celebrated "cabaret" numbers. Photograph courtesy Firoze Rangoonwalla.

ARUNDHATHI SUBRAMANIAM

The future, therefore, becomes difficult to predict, but, as Rahul Srivastava notes, the oscillation between the "Westernized global" and the "revivalist" impulses are likely to grow only more accentuated. Audiences may get to see a lot more "filmi folk", but with a liberal patina of marketable Orientalist chic. Likewise, we are probably equally likely to see a lot more jazz and disco, but invariably juxtaposed with some tribute to the incorruptible soul of Indian culture. (In Subhash Ghai's *Taal*, for instance, it is obvious, that even while mourning a lost cultural innocence, the filmmaker is targeting the very MTV audience that he decries!)

Cultural meteorologists may keep predicting the apocalypse; purists may still dismiss it as mere "running-and-dancing-around-trees". But dance in Hindi cinema continues to cavort on its own whimsical path, blithely irreverent of dire predictions, and never failing to attract its mobs of enthralled viewers, as much today as ever before.

.18
Rekha in Muzaffar Ali's *Umrao Jaan*. Photograph courtesy Firoze Rangoonwalla.

further argue that his slim dark frame, evocative of the male dalit body, is, interestingly, presented in the film as the "modern" body. (In the "Urvasi" song, we are told in no uncertain terms that he with a body as slim as a needle has no reason to visit the chemist – clearly, the celebration of a new aesthetic!)

Dance in Hindi cinema today remains, therefore, the heterogeneous, irrepressibly parodic movement compound that it always was. Dynamic, richly diverse, and flagrantly inconsistent, it seems to revel in defying every definition that one seeks to bestow upon it.

explorations in bharata natyam abroad

Mamata Niyogi-Nakra

The 20th century saw the ebullient blossoming of Indian culture and the arts, coupled as it was with political independence and the emergence of a new nation. The fervour of nation building led to a dramatic development of the arts in all their splendour – rejuvenating the glory of the past and bursting forth into the future. In this exuberance of a youthful nation it was but natural that many new directions emerged in the development of the arts.

This same period also saw the advent of a new world order in which a mushroom growth of technology generated in its wake economic opportunities that resulted in large-scale movement of people. This in turn led to a rapid growth in the number of Indians spread all over the world, loosely referred to as the Indian diaspora. These new waves of emigrants from India were mainly of the middle class, educated and professionals, who carried with them their cultural roots or at least an attachment to them.

Prompted by a desire to maintain their cultural heritage and to reinforce their identity as belonging to an ancient culture and

civilization, Indians of the diaspora have made Bharata Natyam an icon of their heritage. Indian cultural organizations have proliferated abroad, and dancers have been encouraged to impart their art, and through it, their cultural heritage, to those of the new generation born in their new homeland. In this effort they have been aided by the openness of the host societies, who have come to embrace multiculturalism as a mark of their own one-world vision. This article gives a brief summary of the constraints and opportunities in the diaspora that have led to new directions in the evolution of Indian dance.

Bharata Natyam – An International Art

No longer bound by the borders of its country of origin in today's world of freer movement of cultures and people, Indian classical dance, and more particularly Bharata Natyam, has travelled in all directions. It has found niches in far-flung corners of the globe where it is being nurtured collectively with passion and

1
La Troupe Kala Bharati, Montreal, in Bharata Natyam choreographed by Mamata Niyogi-Nakra. Photograph: Michel Nevue.

146

by many; and so, in this new millennium, we can truly affirm that Bharata Natyam has achieved the status of an art form *sans frontières*.

In the 1950s and '60s, some illustrious exponents of Bharata Natyam made significant sorties in the Western world to present their art, which gave Indian dance a recognizable identity. "Lighting lamps in the outer reaches", is how my guru, Shrimati U.K. Chandrabhaga Devi would often describe this mission and act of propagation. The names of Ram Gopal and the couple U.S. Krishna Rao and his wife Chandrabhaga Devi come to mind when speaking of the spread of Bharata Natyam outside India in that period. However, it was mainly in the last quarter of the 20th century that remarkable strides were made in gaining acceptance for Bharata Natyam as a distinct dance style in the Western context.

One of the factors contributing most to this has been the emergence of the Indian diaspora, which has provided a fertile ground for diverse and varied cultural activities. As a

result, dancers trained in India and living in cities all over the world, have set up schools which, besides imparting training in Bharata Natyam, arrange for their students and teachers to give regular performances locally, touring various cities in their regions, and in some instances arranging programmes by visiting artists. The activities of these "local" artists and their cultural institutions have not only helped to create an awareness abroad of the different dance styles of India, but have also provided the sustenance necessary to keep the interest in Indian dance alive after it has been generated. The Indian diaspora has thus

2 and 3
La Troupe Kala Bharati, Montreal, in two sequences from "Seasonscape" choreographed by Mamata Niyogi-Nakra. Creating original contemporary work for the Montreal dance scene, she used Bharata Natyam vocabulary for new patterns in time and space. Photographs: Michel Nevue.

MAMATA NIYOGI-NAKRA

enabled the art of Bharata Natyam to be transplanted outside India and given it the nurturing care needed to ensure its growth and development.

In assessing the interest in Indian dance on the international scene, one cannot ignore the impact of regular tours by exponents of Bharata Natyam from India. These performances by visiting artists, that started a few decades ago and continue in ever increasing numbers, whether government or privately sponsored, have undoubtedly helped to expose Indian dance forms in sometimes virgin territories. Not infrequently, these performers or troupes also undertake to give workshops, lecture-demonstrations, etc., which contribute to a better understanding of the art form. Although a large proportion of these presentations in North America follow the so-called "curry circuit", efforts to move them onto the mainstream scene are beginning to bear fruit, especially in cities in which a more solid and stable base exists, the base being a year-round presence of Indian dance activities over and above the sporadic exposure given by artists on tour.

The Context

Those who undertake the teaching of Bharata Natyam outside the country of origin face formidable challenges. A proper perspective of the context in which this activity is being carried out is necessary to fully understand it. The teachers have to assume a role in which they serve as a conduit through whom the tradition is being passed on and, as well, act as a source of inspiration and encouragement to propel a higher level of achievement. This task is made all the more difficult by the fact that they are teaching Bharata Natyam in a cultural vacuum, as it were. Yet, it is not uncommon to find several exponents of this art, in various cities all over the world, who have taken up this challenge, with some noteworthy results. By adopting methodology and approaches more suited to their circumstances, many teachers from the Indian diaspora have prevailed in successfully imparting the tradition and the art of Bharata Natyam of consistent quality.

4
Rajika Puri (sitting) and Preeti Vasudevan in "Bharatanatyam Variations" explore traditional choreography from a post-modern perspective. They use space, light, colour, and costume to create a contemporary idiom in which tradition speaks today retaining its artistic essence. Photograph: Ken Van Sickle.

5
Trained by Kitappa Pillai in Bharata Natyam, Hari Krishnan, Toronto-based dancer, choreographer, and teacher, performs "dVoid", an abstract movement-oriented solo work inspired by the Buddhist notion of *shunyata*, emptiness. Photograph: Cylla von Tiedemann.

Apart from the commendable contribution of the teachers, a vital and in many ways crucial factor is the support and encouragement their students get from their parents. Many among them start their dance lessons at an early age, almost always at the initiative of their Indian parents. Accordingly, the initial reasons for learning Bharata Natyam are varied, ranging from getting an exposure to Indian culture to being "properly" occupied on Sundays and holidays. Generating an interest in Bharata Natyam as an art form is usually the responsibility of the teacher. This is an important element in the teaching process because without creating that joy and pride in the activity, it will be a

MAMATA NIYOGI-NAKRA

6

In "Revealed by Fire", Lata Pada, a Bharata Natyam exponent and choreographer based in Missasauga, near Toronto, depicts her personal tragedy – the loss of her husband and two daughters in an air accident. When faced with loss, one chooses from one of two roads – to be destroyed by the fire or to allow it to reveal one's hidden strength. Photograph: Cylla von Tiedemann.

fleeting experience, routinely endured and easily dropped. My own experience suggests that it is possible to generate a seriousness of artistic purpose when the teaching is marked by rigour in training and the pursuit of excellence while maintaining strict discipline. By creating such conditions the teacher can help the young students aim and prepare with pride, for their *ranga pravesh*. The pride thus instilled in their achievement propels them to continue their dance activities beyond that

goal. The amount of time and energy such young dancers give to perform on the local dance scene as well as in programmes organized at the community level, can be quite remarkable. Tapping this resource of well-trained and dedicated youngsters, diaspora teachers and choreographers have presented noteworthy dance works, which have impressed the dance lovers of their cities and sometimes impacted on the artistic milieu, both in their own cities as well as elsewhere, including back in India.

Group Choreography in Bharata Natyam

My own experience in this regard has been quite rewarding and I am sure it reflects that of many others in similar situations. Over the years, I have, in Montreal, successfully trained a large number of dancers. However, opportunities to perform Bharata Natyam in the traditional solo format being rather limited, it has been difficult for these accomplished young dancers to get the kind of exposure they deserve. This led me to explore the possibilities of group choreography in Bharata Natyam, pushing my creativity into uncharted space. This creative process in which I have choreographed traditional items as group compositions, where each item required hours of patient group work, would not have been possible without the enthusiastic support of these young dancers. That they all trained with me has, undoubtedly, contributed to a cohesion that is an important quality for group work. This is palpable in their performances and has been noted by critics and connoisseurs alike.

My exploration in group choreography has resulted in a number of evolutionary

changes in my Bharata Natyam presentations. Transforming the solo format into a group composition did not imply merely putting on the stage several dancers, all doing the same movements uniformly as if in a multiple exposure, nor did the choreography follow checkerboard patterning, with one group of dancers doing the movements on the right side and another on the left. Having been exposed to the works of several great Western choreographers, in both ballet and contemporary styles, the patterning took on a new meaning in which four dancers did not only mean four bodies with eight hands and eight legs but also one body with eight hands and eight legs. With this approach it was possible to carve out forms and images in sequences of pure dance movements and create pathways in time and space through formations that reflect the mass and form as well as the geometric and diagrammatic aspects of group choreography.

In this creative process, an equally challenging aspect has been to determine how to make Bharata Natyam, a highly culture-specific dance, accessible to a wider audience. Without compromising the transmission of meaning, I have found it necessary to shift the emphasis from the facial expressions of the individual dancers, to focus on the choreographic panorama. To recreate dance expressions on a larger canvas than the face, thematic interpretations have to be based more on enactment using strident movements of the whole body rather than on gestures of pure narration. Also, movements of pure dance in Bharata Natyam, considered bereft of meaning, have been used to communicate emotions in choreographic patterns that heighten ambience

and effectively transmit the underlying message of the choreographic work. Undeniably, my personal exposure to Western thinking on group choreography has prompted me to go beyond the conventional and explore the possibilities that Bharata Natyam has to offer. This philosophy of looking at the expressiveness of a group of bodies has been aptly enunciated by Michel Fokine in his now famous letter to *The Times*, London (July 6, 1914) proposing the five principles of reform in ballet. He wrote: "The group is not only an ornament. The new ballet advances from the expressiveness of the face and the hands to that of the whole body, and from that of the individual body to groups of bodies and the expressiveness of the combined dancing of a crowd." Interestingly, a similar trend in thinking has also been noticed in the work of some choreographers in India.

Group presentations in Indian dance styles are nowadays commonly seen in the works of many dance teachers of the diaspora, not only in North America but in other parts of the world as well, all within their own cultural bowers.

Fusion and Other Initiatives

It must be noted that most of the diaspora artists have exposure to a large body of dance work in the mainstream. This fact, coupled with their needs and resources, has led them into various other directions: some have choreographed dance pieces in fusion with some Western dance styles while others have shared their creative process with Western choreographers. Kathak and Flamenco fusion has taken place in some productions and in others Bharata Natyam with modern dance; the fusion in some instances being merely juxtaposition. Another noticeable trend has been to juxtapose different Indian dance styles in formations. Equally noteworthy are the choices made by these dancers in presenting non-traditional themes with relevance to contemporary or social issues.

My own initiative in fusion has been to choreograph Bharata Natyam with all its characteristic movements to the accompaniment of jazz and the reading of haiku, in a piece called "Dansjazz-ku". As Vincent Warren, in his review in *Sruti* magazine put it, this piece "delicately balanced diverse disciplines from both the Western and Asian cultures.... The abhinaya used here asked for subtle gestures and facial expressions... [and the choreographer] has not betrayed the principles of Bharatanatyam.... In fact she has shown the power of this dance-form to transcend cultural barriers and speak of moods and emotions common to all humanity."

Mainstreaming Initiatives

Significant forays in new directions have sometimes been made by Indian dance choreographers when they have had to share billings with choreographers of different

7
"Revealed by Fire" is a collaborative work. Dramaturg Judakoff, photographer Cylla von Tiedemann, music composer Timothy Sullivan, and choreographer Lata Pada and her Sampradaya Dance Creations' artists worked together celebrating a woman's journey of transformation forged in unspeakable tragedy. Photograph: Andrew Oxenham.

backgrounds, at dance festivals or forums. Such occasions have incited a fresh look at the possibilities that Indian classical dance has to offer, and have provided challenges to the diaspora artists for new creations, blending their work with the evening's other presentations while remaining true to their tradition. Such creations generally get a more contemporary treatment.

An example of such contemporary treatment in Bharata Natyam, from my own experience, was the creation of "Seasonscape", which was a result of an invitation for me from Tangente, a mainstream dance organization in Montreal, to participate in a series of productions which involved presenting six choreographers of different training and background, all working on the theme of "seasons". I had to come up with a piece using the idiom of Bharata Natyam that would reflect the mandate of Tangente productions, which was to create original contemporary works for the Montreal dance scene. Using the vocabulary of Bharata Natyam, new patterns were created in space and time, capturing the symphony of colours of the seasons in India as I remembered them from my childhood days. The music was strictly classical Carnatic vocal, composed and sung by none other than Madurai T.N. Seshagopalan, without words, yet evoking the thoughts expressed in the haiku verses I had written in English, that formed the basis of the choreography. The costumes were patterned on Bharata Natyam but modified to suit the piece and its movements.

The reception that has been accorded to "Seasonscape", both in its place of origin and also back in India, exemplifies how the seeds of Bharata Natyam sown in an alien but

8
Minnesota-based Odissi exponent Ananya Chatterjea in "Women of Lost Homes", 2002. Inspired by the struggles of women across the world whose children have "disappeared" as a result of political violence, this piece draws on the practice of *rudaali*, ritual mourning by women in rural India. Danced to the poetry of Faiz Ahmad Faiz and scored by Nusrat Fateh Ali Khan. Photograph: Erik Saulitis.

9
"Making Rain", choreographed by Ananya Chatterjea, 2002. Danced to the Sufi song by Reshma, the piece works through lament, fury, pleading, disappointment, and ultimately reaches towards hope. It is inspired by the untiring work of women leaders in peace movements. Photograph: Erik Saulitis.

hospitable and fertile environment have not only taken root but decidedly flourished and blossomed in splendour. "Seasonscape", performed by la Troupe Kala Bharati of Montreal, was recorded by the Central Production Centre of Doordarshan in Delhi in December 1997 and telecast in August '98 on the national network as part of the closing ceremonies of the fiftieth anniversary of Indian Independence.

Evolution of Bharata Natyam in the Cultural Bower
Underlying the recognition such successful efforts have gained, there is a realization that these creations are born out of demands on choreographers working in the Indian cultural bower within host cultures that are often contradictory. While on the one hand it is important to maintain the authenticity of the tradition, on the other, it is necessary to

present it in such a way as to not seem forbidding. In their attempt to uphold tradition and preserve the art with earnestness and enthusiasm, the diaspora dancers run the risk of freezing Bharata Natyam in their own time-frames. Equally detrimental to the practice of their art would be to succumb to undue pressures in search of newness just for the sake of innovation, without real artistic merit. By maintaining a fine balance of the two – tradition and experimentation – new directions have been given that have resulted in a remarkable evolution of Bharata Natyam in the cultural bower that is the diaspora.

growths
and outgrowths

Sanjoy Roy

Indian dance has long been present in the UK, seeded by visitors and grown by settlers. Uday Shankar first performed with Anna Pavlova in the 1920s, later setting up his own company in Dartington Hall, Devon. From the late 1930s, Ram Gopal enraptured audiences with his brilliance and showmanship. And with the large-scale migration of people from the Indian subcontinent during the '50s and '60s, and later Indians from East Africa during the early '70s, there arrived a larger pool of dancers who settled in the UK.

For some time, Indian dance was seen simply as a foreign import, like some lush hothouse plant that evoked wonder and perplexity – a non-native species. For migrant communities too, Indian dance could symbolize and affirm a heritage, a past, a sense of identity from elsewhere. More recently, with the growth of substantial numbers of British-born Indians, that sense of identity has shifted emphasis – or rather, has become more diverse. The seeds that were planted have grown wayward offshoots, bloomed unpredictably, and borne strange fruit. Some practitioners have sought to reaffirm their roots, while others turned away, finding them inadequate as a means of expression. Some were attracted by the form and precision of classical dance; others experimented with that form in a quest for a more individual style. Some were concerned with preservation, with technique, with tradition, while others were more interested in innovation, in experiment, and exploration.

Given this history, it is hardly surprising that issues of identity, community, and authenticity have been a particularly strong focus for debates (and arguments) around defining and evaluating Indian dance in the UK, especially when it comes to looking at "new directions" in the art form. Often these debates hinge on particular ideas of classicism, tradition, heritage, and relevance, in relation to the appropriateness and quality for the subject, style, and theme, to the choices of music and costume, to the technical skills of the dancers and their methods of training.

While such questions are interesting and valuable for audiences, commentators, and critics, the most successful and innovative of the new Indian dance works in the UK have – in my opinion – emerged from dancers and choreographers experimenting with the medium of dance itself: the movement and placement of human bodies on stage, the interaction with music and design. To be sure, their work raises issues in relation to identity and community – but that seems more often an effect than an intention of their choreography.

The point is illustrated by two very different artists working in this field: Shobana Jeyasingh and Akram Khan. Utterly different in temperament and style, they have both garnered considerable critical acclaim, and both have the exploration of movement as their base. I focus on these two here, partly in the interests of giving depth, and partly

1
Akram Khan in "Loose in Flight" (1996). Trained by London-based Pratap Pawar, a disciple of Pandit Birju Maharaj, Akram has studied traditional classical Kathak and presented it with great success. Photograph: Allan F. Parker.

because they are as yet the only two choreographers in this area to have achieved mainstream critical success.

Shobana Jeyasingh originally trained in Bharata Natyam in India and Malaysia, and toured for several years as a solo performer in this style. She formed her own company in 1988, and stopped dancing in 1991 to focus on choreography. Wishing to move away from the securities of classical form, she began experimenting with the style, and produced her first piece, "Configurations" in 1988. She used elemental components – clear lines and directions, defined body shapes and rhythmically articulate footwork – and reconfigured the traditionally solo form into an ensemble piece for four dancers. Using formal devices of repetition and variation in time and space – a compositional method that accorded well with the commissioned score for string quartet by minimalist composer Michael Nyman – "Configurations" created a sparkling, crystalline geometry of movement.

"Making of Maps" (1992) and "Romance...with Footnotes" (1993) were

2–5

"Kaash" (If), the latest choreographic work by Akram Khan. Following training in contemporary dance, he further extended his dance vocabulary, drawing from classical Kathak and soon emerged as a gifted choreographer. He astounds his audiences with his distinctive style of quick-fire motion. Photographs: Roy Peters.

significant developments from this "analytical" mode, Jeyasingh varying Bharata Natyam derived movement much more widely. A moment from "Romance...with Footnotes" summarizes her intent: a pair of dancers, one adopting a classical pose with the other slowly circling her, as if inspecting the stance, then gently pulling her off-centre to see what happens, how she moves. The effect was like seeing statues shifted from their pedestals and given waywardly human form. Both "Making of Maps" and "Romance...with Footnotes" explore this tension between classical and personal styles, alternating between the precision of Bharata Natyam and more waywardly idiosyncratic movement.

"Raid" (1995) marked a further development. Taking inspiration from the Indian game kabbadi, Jeyasingh set two types of movement against each other – dance and sport – the two "teams" edgily making forays into each other's territories. It was a liberating piece for Jeyasingh: using sports movements freed her from the constraints of classical dance, hitherto the central reference point of her choreography, and opened up a greater spatial and dynamic range.

"Palimpsest" (1996) showed her savouring this new-found freedom. More intriguingly complex than previous works, with a wider

6
Akram Khan and Mavin Khoo in "No Male Egos". Photograph: Peter Teigen.

SANJOY ROY

7
Chitra Srishailan in "Surface
Tension", choreographed by
Shobana Jeyasingh.
Photograph: Chris Nash.

of movement, here they are interwoven in variegated, overlapping phrases.

"Palimpsest" marks the beginning of Jeyasingh's mature style. From here onwards, Jeyasingh seems confident enough to take movements from a variety of sources, and then to tamper, break, or mould them according to her own concerns. Whereas in "Making of Maps" and "Romance...with Footnotes" there was a suggestion of a dialogue between classical and contemporary movement, since "Palimpsest" her works have been more like multiple voices speaking at once, or inventing new languages. There has also been a heightened sense of tension, density, and speed. Increasingly, in "Intimacies of a Third Order" (1998) and then "Fine Frenzy" (1999), Jeyasingh has asked her dancers to incorporate rapid-fire shifts in style and pace, to interrupt flows of movement and shape with sudden cuts and freezes. "Surface Tension" (2000) again showed jagged breaks in flow and direction, but then quietened to a gentler and more sensual mood – and for the first time, Jeyasingh used filmed projections within a stage work.

Jeyasingh commissions contemporary music for her work, notably from Michael Nyman, Kevin Volans, Glynn Perrin, Graham Fitkin, and Django Bates. Several times she has used scores which mix together an Indian and a Western composition, for example "Making of Maps" (Alistair Macdonald with R.A. Ramamani), "Rapid" (Perrin with Ilayaraaja).

The designs she uses tend to be bold and simple, based on shape and colour and leaving ample space for the dance. Notable designs include Belinda Ackerman's starkly effective

dynamic range and more sophisticated use of stage space, it is nevertheless, characteristically, a tightly structured piece, its phrases repeated and varied in a sequence of abstract episodes. It draws on diverse movement sources, including *nritta*, *abhinaya*, the martial arts Chhau and Kalaripayattu, naturalistic gesture, and idiosyncratic movement invention. Unlike in "Raid", where contrasting styles appear as distinctive blocks

162

set for "Romance...with Footnotes", and Keith Khan's strikingly inventive sets and costumes for "Raid" and "Palimpsest". More recently she has collaborated several times with set designer Madeleine Morris and costume designer Ursula Bombshell, both of whom have contributed considerably to the "look" of her current company. While her set designs have always had a modernist feel, it was only since "Palimpsest" that her costumes have moved significantly away from referencing Indian-style clothing, becoming bolder and more streamlined.

A choreographer of keen intellect, Jeyasingh was for many years the pre-eminent artist in the field of "contemporary" Indian dance in the UK. She spawned imitators, admirers, and detractors, and she was undoubtedly a powerful force in energizing the scene. But until recently, none approached her artistic status or garnered her critical acclaim. Now Akram Khan – a wholly different persona from Jeyasingh, and from a younger generation – is currently forging his own distinctive path. While Jeyasingh was trained in Bharata Natyam, in India and Malaysia, Khan trained in Kathak, in the UK. Jeyasingh's choreographic career took off when she stopped dancing herself, while Khan's is currently developing around his own performances. And whereas Jeyasingh's initial experiments were with ensemble forms and structures, only later developing new movement vocabularies, Khan began with those explorations as a solo performer, questions of group composition arising from that base.

Khan is still in the early stages of his dance career, but has caught the attention of critics. In 1996, when he was only 21, he

performed a Kathak solo and a remarkably assured contemporary composition, "Loose in Flight", an inventive and compelling solo which was later made into a short film for Channel 4 television. It shows Khan breaking away from and returning to a single, centred Kathak position. Between these fixed points, the position at times collapses and breaks, so that Khan appears like an energized puppet alternately cutting loose from and being reined in by its strings. Like Jeyasingh in her earlier days, but to wholly different effect, Khan here seemed to be interrogating the classical tradition of his training, investigating his points of departure and return.

"Fix" (2000), another solo, is set to Nitin Sawhney's coolly urban score, short riffs, and fleeting themes gusting across the stage, underpinned by sparse but funky rhythms. Khan, dressed in loose white, moves slowly across the front of the stage. Then he, too, develops his own riffs, playing with the dynamics of tension and release. From tracing a tight, knotty spiral with his arms, he suddenly drops into casual crouched bounces, arms swinging easily. Or, like a spring uncoiling, he whips a laconic turn into a series of dizzying spins which topples him over to tumble across the floor.

Khan has an astonishing stage presence, as rivetting to watch when motionless as during his mercurial flashes of speed. And whereas the restraining puppet strings seem almost tangible in "Loose in Flight", "Fix" shows Khan in full command of himself: at the closing moment, he mimes lifting his own knee by a wire, and then casually releases it.

"Rush" (2000) is Khan's first group choreography. Performed with contemporary

163

dancers Gwyn Emberton and Moya Michael, the piece is stamped with Khan's distinctive style of quickfire motion within fluctuating cycles of tension and reverberation. The work is even tauter than "Fix" and darker in tone, the dancers dressed in black against a bare, dimly-lit stage, Andy Cowton providing a driven, machine-like score. It's inspired by paragliders in freefall, but there's nothing literal to suggest that theme. Instead, there is the suspense between speed and stillness – admirably suited to Khan's movement concerns – and there are intimations of wings and wind, or the triangular shape of a kite. A sudden flash of blue light starts off the motion, as if the dancers had fallen from a plane; later, Moya Michael whirls her arms as rapidly and rigidly as propeller blades.

The construction is tight and formal, phrases passed between the dancers, duets and trios splintering out of phase, interlocking and reforming. In the end the work is more interesting for Khan's idiosyncratic movement invention than for its composition – Khan is still most powerful as a soloist. But judging from his work to date, this young dancer/ choreographer is set to go far.

Earlier in 2000, Khan took part in a choreographic project with Mavin Khoo, a Bharata Natyam dancer. Called "No Male Egos", the piece showcased their contrasting talents (which made something of a mismatch when they performed together). Khoo is a well known performer in his own right. He has a strong Bharata Natyam technique, and has also trained in ballet with Merce Cunningham.

Khoo has made his own contemporary compositions, for example "Cast in Stone?" (2000), a duet for himself and Christopher

Bannerman that sets up a series of striking contrasts. Bannerman is much older than Khoo, and his training is in contemporary dance. He performs fully clothed, while Khoo performs wearing only black trunks. And in all the duets, Bannerman is the supporter, while Khoo balances in position. The piece is based on ideas of animating sculpture, and in a bold move into new territory, Khoo performs it in ballet pointe shoes. Supported by Bannerman, he moves slowly between poses adapted from temple friezes, his body tensed into elongated stretches and balances. The choreographic tensions set up are not only created by the contrasts between the two performers, but also by suggestions of an intriguing interplay between sculptor, sculpture, and human flesh. A compelling piece, it nevertheless feels more like a study based on a particular idea rather than a fully realized piece of choreography.

Khoo has also performed with Sankalpam, a group of dancers trained in Bharata Natyam. Like Angika, and indeed many other Indian dance groups, Sankalpam works with various thematic ideas while remaining largely within a classical Indian dance vocabulary. Unusual among these is perhaps Wise Thoughts dance company, notable for its issue-based work around themes of homosexuality, gay identity, and HIV awareness.

This chapter has focused on two particular choreographers, Jeyasingh and Khan, because of all the new "offshoots" in Indian dance that have emerged in the UK, these two have gone the furthest and been the most artistically convincing in establishing and developing a

9
Mavin Khoo executes an exquisite *utplavana*, jump movement in "Parallel Passions" (2001), a work commissioned by the Royal Opera House Artists' Development Initiative, London. Photograph: Eric Richmond.

personal style, to the extent that they are most readily identifiable not as "Indian dancers", but as their individual selves.

Still, numerous other styles of work continue to be made, and other choreographers of stature will doubtless emerge. It is interesting to note, however, that both Khan and Jeyasingh have developed their styles from the *nritta* strand of Indian dance, and as yet there has been no established trend deriving from the more narrative *abhinaya* aspect of the tradition.

One critically neglected arena that deserves special mention is popular dance. Since the bhangra explosion in the 1980s, Indi-pop dance has also embraced the pumping hips and glitzy shimmies of filmi dance on the one hand, and the cool-dude attitude of rap and reggae on the other. This "new direction" in Indian dance is certainly here to stay – though where it will lead is anyone's guess. More concerned with image, pose, and pleasure than with authenticity or artistry, popular dance gleefully hybridizes its moves, steps, and looks, aiming more for style than statement. (I look forward to the day when theatre dance can achieve the same degree of freedom.)

Finally no commentary on Indian dance in the UK can avoid mentioning "Coming of Age", under the artistic direction of Keith Khan, performed on two consecutive evenings in August 2000 outside the Royal Festival Hall in London. Organized by Akademi (formerly the Academy of Indian Dance) to mark its 21st birthday, this large-scale celebration cast a magical carnival spell. Ram Gopal himself took pride of place at one end of the performing space, looking across the several

generations of dancers participating – a veritable melange of multifarious styles. While some performed their finely-honed classical moves from Bharata Natyam, Kathak, and Odissi, others hiked up their legs in balletic kicks, or spun ecstatically towards a place where Kathak meets club dance. For anyone who wished to see how the seeds of Indian dance have grown in the UK, this celebration provided an unforgettable vision of its multifarious branches, curling tendrils, and weird efflorescences.

reinscribing "indian" dance

Uttara Asha Coorlawala

The issue of what constitutes contemporary Indian dance generated controversies at the choreography workshop entitled "New Directions In Indian Dance", organized by Georg Lechner in New Delhi in September 1993. The controversies exemplified some of the perceptions, pitfalls, possibilities with which new Indian dance must contend, as well as the excitement that has accompanied its reception.

In accordance with the organizer's intent, a small group of like-minded "innovators" engaged in dialogue among themselves about choreographic problems in private sessions during the day, while at night public performances of new works played to packed houses. However, the organizer was criticized and the event denounced in the New Delhi press for excluding major dance figures of the classical ilk and several critics. "Did the omission of all the classical dancers imply that creativity was the forte of innovative modern dancers alone?" and "Who are these foreigners trying to tell us what Indian dance should be?"

In his response, Lechner clarified his view: one more national event that provided representation to plural and clashing views on creativity would defeat the purpose of a "workshop" which was meant to focus closely on methods and techniques of evolving new directions in choreography. His concern was not with creativity within Indian dance, but with supporting and developing departures from the specific traditional criteria of classical dance, departures that expanded aesthetic and political boundaries. Thus excluded were classical dancers of star status who also had innovated but well within their defined territories. Similarly, excluded were dance critics whose evaluative visions were based on exclusively classical criteria.

Innovative choreographers argue that classical dance as imprinted upon themselves, and as performed today, is loaded with personal, nationalistic, and intercultural hegemonic investments. They express dissent through subversive choices and departures from prevailing models of performance. Their works vary from being socially reactive, structure-based, gender oriented to personal expressions of a spiritual search.

There persists among Indian dance enthusiasts an Orientalistic perception that the

1
"Chairpiece", choreographed by Gary Davis. In this avant garde dance Uttara Asha Coorlawala develops a "very personal relationship" with a chair as she twists herself around, under, and on it. Photograph: Subodh Chandra.

UTTARA ASHA COORLAWALA

criteria of classical dance are immutable with unchanging formulae; that classical dance is an inheritance from antiquity somehow frozen in an eternal present. As a deliberate strategy, the fostering of this perception accomplished two ends successfully. First, it re-assigned the ownership of these formulae from upstart interpreters to the original owners of the traditions, to the lineages of teachers who have always danced or taught dance, and to those exponents who have been imprinted for years by the practice of a form. Secondly the tactic demanded that beyond India, critics of dance unfamiliar with Indian classical dance either acquaint themselves with the complexities of the form or desist from making authoritative statements about it. The drawback of this strategy on an international level, however, was that classical dances were either mystified and exoticized, or ignored as art dance and re-presented as ethnic (read social, non-specialist). In contrast, innovative Indian choreographers have been celebrated in Britain, Europe, and the USA on alternative dance or more centrally positioned venues. To an extent then, the proponents of change and creativity within tradition – protesting their exclusion from this small but significant workshop – were protesting being identified with constructs of their own making.

While traditional criteria are constantly being reinterpreted, critics evaluate ongoing performances, endorse or reject the creative choices made within the frames of the classical tradition, and so participate in the reinscription of the "traditionally Indian." In addition to dances that faithfully reconstruct inherited movements and forms, no doubt there are dances that innovate within

boundaries of form; dances that adapt or "translate" traditional elements for the urban public and proscenium theatres; dances that extend the borders of the classical forms; and multilingual dances that dialogue with modernity and internationalism, that reflect the churning fast-paced changes in Indian society. However, the critics and dancers who protested at their exclusion from the above "New Directions" workshop chose, for this occasion only, not to distinguish between innovations within and beyond "tradition".

As Erdman has pointed out, "the artist's role in a transitional period is subject to criticism from those whose perspectives offer a different view of the transitional issues."[1]

The Indian press prior to the mid-1990s also participated extensively in inscribing and defining "Indian dance".[2] The politics of dancers, of representation, of procedures for selecting dancers for festivals, of trumped up aesthetic controversies and personal investments have often taken precedence in the allotment of printed space over factual analysis and description of the art itself – suggesting thereby that the star status of dancers is more interesting than what they dance. Editorial policies have tended to ignore inter-influences, and to encourage the drama of dichotomizing aesthetic differences between artists. This led to a notion that some kind of conceptual war exists between the proponents of traditional and post-traditional dance.

Defining Indian dance is crucial, for it empowers those works and performers included within the definitions and marginalizes the creative works that fall beyond the prescribed categories. It is generally accepted that a critic or observer

2
"Deep Inside" is the second part of a trilogy of songs composed by Nada Clyne and set to dance in the style of ecstatic *padam*s by Uttara. Photograph: Stuart Roth.

steeped in the very specific aesthetics of classical ballet, modern dance of the 1960s, or of classical Indian dance, evaluates through a particular grid of constructs. However, in the case of innovative presentations involving intercultural elements, critical responses often focus only upon the culturally approved aspects and ignore the subversive and often newer aspects of the work. What is not recognized is often rendered non-existent in terms of the written or verbal record. For example, the introduction of any movement systems unfamiliar to a dance critic or casual observer, even if based on a non-dance element within the same culture, such as yoga in India, evokes a non-response or is received as a blur of unidentified non-specific movement images.

Though pan-Indian characteristics are assumed in much of today's discourse within the urban cultural centres in India, administrators, particularly those concerned with projecting India's culture abroad have bemoaned the lack of specific and appropriate criteria for evaluating and for describing what is "Indian" about the Indian classical forms. Investments in nationalism, recovery of archaic practices, reclamation, search for cultural identity, need for international approbation and accessibility, need to incorporate the newest

3–5
Sequences from "Ushas Sukta", choreographed by Mohanrao Kalyanpurkar, based on a hymn from the *Rigveda*. Photographs: Stuart Roth.

UTTARA ASHA COORLAWALA

international trends, have all factored in on determinations as to which dances should be seen internationally as representative of Indian culture. Often tradition is equated with nationalism, the status quo is reaffirmed, and profound changes are resisted as expressions of Western (read anti-national) influence.

Centuries of reinscriptions of the criteria of Indian dance arts range from the *Natyashastra* to danced and written descriptions of what was seen by the early performers from the West (Ruth St Denis, La Meri, Ragini Devi, Faubian Bowers), from the nationalistic constructs of visionary revivalists as Vallathol, Rukmini Devi, Uday Shankar, and Ananda Kentish Coomaraswamy, and recent

6
"Amrit", choreographed by Uttara to music by Stanley B. Sussman. Photograph: Subodh Chandra.

7
"Yaksha", presented at the Unesco festival in Bombay in 1977 shows Uttara's early choreography combining Bharata Natyam and modern dance to the music of Anand Shankar. Photograph: Rajdatt.

8
"Mirroirs". This contemplative abstract work by Sun Ock Lee is based on qualities of movement in Korean traditional dance and set to the music of Ravel. Photograph: Subodh Chandra.

translations of old texts, to authoritative descriptions of classical Indian forms by the scholars Joan Erdman, Mohan Khokar, Sunil Kothari, V. Raghavan, S.K. Saxena, Kapila Vatsyayan, Phillip Zarilli, and of course the writings of dance critics – Sadanand Menon, Shanta Serbjeet Singh, Subuddu, Leela Venkataraman, and others.

Lucid, passionate articles on issues on different facets of classical dance forms with a particular focus on Bharata Natyam and Carnatic music in the monthly magazine *Sruti* have opened a way to discuss complexity without mystification, and to honour lineages of dance teachers without appropriating their livelihoods, or belittling their remarkable contribution in sustaining continuity in the dance forms through centuries. Since the articles are in English with transliterated technical terms, they are accessible internationally. Most recently, Ashish Khokar's series of annuals on dance titled *AttenDance* have offered a counter vision to the Sanskritic perspective of Indianness in dance.

Thus the constant process of reinscriptions continues, with each generation focusing either on what was silenced in previous narratives, or responding to changing paradigms of perception. Amid scholars and innovative choreographers, de-colonizing, deconstructive, and post-modern perspectives are replacing formulaic conventions and Orientalist representations of otherness. While changing paradigms instigate new insights and re-empowerment, they also raise fresh intercultural issues: for example *bhakti*, formerly considered an empowering subversive practice, becomes a vehicle of patriarchy; cross-gendered representations give way to gender-specific role-playing. Contemporary dancers insist that yoga be respected as an empirically developed system basic to development of skills rather than as a theoretic part of Indological literature or as esoteric mysticism.

Increasing numbers of exponents of each genre of Indian dance are spread across the globe today, whose personal investments in dancing vary tremendously. The notion of a single aesthetic of Indianness ignores accumulations of diverse aesthetic considerations. The rich ferment of activities (*manthan*) within the dance in India cannot be forced to yield neat conclusions for scholars to latch on to and cite. Nor can there be a neutral dialogue as long as artists and scholars are busy establishing individual domains of creativity and influence through each interaction. It is time to abandon such fictions masking the surface of change.

Notes

This article is an abbreviated version of a part of my dissertation at New York University in 1994.

1. Joan Erdman, *Patrons and Performers in Rajasthan*, New Delhi, Chanakya Publications, 1985, p. 180.

2. The press has since preferred to focus on mass media events, televized narratives, Indian films and film stars.

In this section we present a selection of the works of a few dancers/choreographers who have been active on the scene and part of the ongoing movement of Indian dance seeking new directions and attempting innovative and experimental works. Offered here is a glimpse into what is happening concurrently with classical dance practice.

During the Uday Shankar Centenary celebrations (2001–02) a series of dance festivals was arranged by the Sangeet Natak Akademi in New Delhi, Chennai, and Kolkata, showcasing dancers working in the area of new directions in Indian dance. Dancers and choreographers from the new generation shared a platform with their established and senior counterparts. A similar selection is attempted here.

Besides those featured here, several other dancers are also active on the scene, including Sudarshan Chakravorty (Sapphire Creations), Kolkata; Ananda Shankar Jayant, Hyderabad; Ratnabali Kant with her group, New Delhi; Tripura Kashyap (Apoorva Dance Theatre), Bangalore; Santosh Nair (Sadhya), New Delhi; Madhu Nataraj-Heri (Stem Dance Theatre), Bangalore; and Bharat Sharma (Bhoorang), Bangalore.

The photographs in this section reveal another face of the Indian dance scene.

- Sunil Kothari

A CROSS-SECTION OF CHOREOGRAPHIC WORKS

Mallika Sarabhai had enviable exposure and opportunities to work with her mother Mrinalini in several choreographic works, and emerged in her own right as a brilliant performer and choreographer. She expanded her dance vocabulary by studying the martial arts of south India and northeast India, drawing on everyday movements and gestures, thus crystallizing what it was she wanted to express through her work.

She created pieces that reacted to communal violence in India: "Mean Streets on Earth" and "V for...".

In her role as Draupadi in Peter Brook's "Mahabharata", Mallika became aware of the need to make strong and positive statements about the representation of Indian women. It led her to create "Shakti – the Power of Women" in which she attempted reappraisals of mythological, historical, and contemporary female characters. Its unprecedented success led to a second piece "Sita's Daughters" about women who refuse to accept an oppressive system.

She teamed up with Nigerian performer Peter Badejo in "Itan Kahani – The Story of Stories" and its sequel "Itan Kahani – 2" in which they used dialogues and acting, dance and mime, computers and e-mail to tell stories of gods, icons, and cultural symbols of our times.

In 2002 she choreographed a collaborative work titled "The Journey Inward: Devi Mahatmya". Mallika recites from American poet Suzanne Ironbiter's long poem invoking Durga, and performs with her troupe to the musical score by Mark and Philipe Haydon with rock compositions complementing actual and figurative combative moods. With sets by Jodie Fried – including huge masts swung about by breezes – and costumes also by her, the work stands out for its power, spectacle, and multi-layered presentation.

1

"Mean Streets on Earth": Mallika Sarabhai portrays an ordinary situation – a woman walking on the street with no idea that she will be attacked. Photograph courtesy Darpana Academy of Performing Arts, Ahmedabad.

178

2
"V for...": Mallika changes costumes quickly as she enters the skin of the characters, driving home the point that we have become insensitive to the violence all around us. Photograph courtesy Darpana Academy of Performing Arts, Ahmedabad.

3
"Itan Kahani – 2" choreographed by Mallika Sarabhai and Peter Badejo. Photograph courtesy Darpana Academy of Performing Arts, Ahmedabad.

4
In "Devi Mahatmya", the ritualistic practice and the power of Devi are presented in spectacular and meaningful manner. Photograph courtesy Darpana Academy of Performing Arts, Ahmedabad.

Aditi Mangaldas, trained in Kathak by Kumudini Lakhia and Birju Maharaj, has choreographed a number of solo and group ensembles, both traditional and contemporary, for her Drishtikon Dance Foundation, New Delhi. They reflect the spirit of Kathak and go beyond its form and content to create a new language.

1
"Movement and Space", an extract from "Hidden Stream": Aditi Mangaldas uses Kathak, Chhau, and yoga to unfurl the potential of the body and to create a visualscape that adheres to no particular rule. Mini Thaper in yoga, Aditi in Kathak, and Santosh Nair in Chhau. Photograph: Dinesh Khanna, courtesy Drishtikon Dance Foundation.

2

"Rhythm and Sound", an extract from "Hidden Stream": It explores vibrant sounds that echo through dance, discovers silent rhythms, goes beyond traditional footwork to find new expressions of rhythm and sound. Different textured floors and an unusual spectrum of props enhance the effect. As the sound of the beat reaches the ear the body begins to respond and becomes the instrument, resonating with the rhythm, creating new patterns and painting new soundscapes. Photograph: Dinesh Khanna, courtesy Drishtikon Dance Foundation.

3

"Grishma (Summer)", a sequence from "Footprints on Water": "The fire within me consumes the fire outside of me." Choreographed and danced solo by Aditi Mangaldas. Photograph: John Panikar.

Maulik Shah and **Ishira Parikh**, the husband and wife team, were trained in Kathak by Kumudini Lakhia. They took part in Kumudini's major choreographic works for a number of years. They now run Anarta, an academy of Kathak in Ahmedabad. Both have choreographed several innovative and experimental works in Kathak, using contemporary Indian poetry and abstract themes, and have toured within India and abroad.

1
Maulik Shah presents the theme of time, as a solo, attired as a young man of today, using several elements of Kathak in a creative manner, with the narrative in English. Photograph courtesy Anarta Academy of Kathak Dance.

1, and 2-4 (*following pages*) Sequences from "The Sound of Silence", choreographed and directed by Madhu Gopinath and Vakkom Sajeev. Photographs courtesy Samudra Centre for Indian Contemporary Performing Arts; photographs 2 and 4 by Sathyan.

After their four-year association with Daksha Sheth's Aarti Dance Company and Kosh Company (UK) for one year, **Madhu Gopinath** and **Vakkom Sajeev** formed Samudra Centre for Indian Contemporary Performing Arts at Thiruvananthapuram. Trained in Bharata Natyam, Kalaripayattu, yoga, mallkhamb, and gymnastics they have created interesting choreographic works drawing upon the traditional dance forms and related physical traditions of Kerala.

Anita Ratnam had her initial training in Bharata Natyam supplemented by Kathakali and Mohini Attam. After a ten-year stay in New York, she returned to India and established Arangham Dance Theatre in Chennai. She performs within the country and abroad, also collaborating with artists from abroad. The Other Festival, an annual event organized by Anita Ratnam and Ranvir Shah in Chennai is a major platform for contemporary works.

1
Anita Ratnam explores elements of contact improvisation with dancers of her Arangham Dance Theatre in "Daughters of the Ocean", based on Shobita Punja's text using *vachikabhinaya*, directly talking to audiences about key events from her life.
Photograph: C.P. Satyajit.

2
A sequence from "Dust", focusing on the kinetic and aesthetic potential of mixing Bharata Natyam and contemporary post-modern movement forms, choreographed by Anita Ratnam in collaboration with Mark Taylor of Dance Alloy, Pittsburgh, USA. Photograph: Vipul Sangoi.

3
A sequence from "Gajaanana", performed at the Uday Shankar Shatabdi Samaroha, Kolkata, 2002. Anita uses diverse traditional dance forms to narrate the story of the birth of Ganapati. Photograph: T.R. Narayanswamy, courtesy Arangham Dance Theatre.

1
In "Gandhari – Ek Pratibimb" from the epic Mahabharata, choreographed by Sangeeta Sharma, two images of Gandhari represent the contradictions she faced in her life, finally merging into a third figure, destined for a tragic end. Photograph courtesy Sangeeta Sharma.

Sangeeta Sharma trained in Indian contemporary dance under Narendra Sharma at Bhoomika Creative Dance Centre, New Delhi where she is now a senior Ballet Master. She has choreographed several independent works.

Sharmila Biswas, trained by Guru Kelucharan Mahapatra in Odissi, is based in Kolkata and heads the Odissi Vision and Movement Centre. Using classical Odissi technique, she has explored Oriya drum traditions and through group work attempted contemporary interpretations of traditional themes. She has also dealt with the issue of the Maharis, the temple dancers of Orissa, inviting a traditional Mahari to perform with her group.

1
A sequence from "Dhulikhel", choreographed by Sharmila Biswas, celebrating the joy of life to the accompaniment of drums. Photograph: Satyaki Ghosh.

Ileana Citaristi, an Italian dancer and exponent of Odissi and Mayurbhanj Chhau, is based in Bhubaneswar. Trained by Guru Kelucharan Mahapatra in Odissi, by Shri Hari in Mayurbhanj Chhau, and also by other traditional masters, she continues to create innovative choreography and has extended her work to choreographing sequences for a few Indian films, winning national awards.

1
Ileana Citaristi explores the form of Mayurbhanj Chhau to interpret the Greek myth of Narcissus and Echo, choreographed by her with a distinct dance vocabulary. Photograph courtesy Ileana Citaristi.

Navtej Singh Johar is a performer and choreographer whose work ranges from classical Bharata Natyam to performance-art, street theatre, and performance installations. He has worked with Chandralekha, Leela Samson, Justine McCarthy, and abroad with Peter Sparling, Janet Lilly in New York, and the Akademi in the UK. He is based in New Delhi and runs Studio Abhyas offering training in Bharata Natyam, yoga and related physical traditions.

1
In his choreographic work "The Place of Path", Navtej Singh Johar draws from a variety of images from Eastern traditions that express the austere and the sensual, and successfully uses improvisation and *abhinaya*. Photograph courtesy Studio Abhyas.

1
A sequence from "Beyond the Walls for Men", an Indo-European collaborative project, exploring various dance elements including martial arts and contemporary dance. Photograph: Hugo Glendinning.

Jayachandran Palazhy, a leading choreographer and dancer of the young generation, trained in Bharata Natyam under Kalamandalam Kshemavathy and the Dhananjayans, and studied Kathakali at Kalakshetra. He also received lessons in Kalaripayattu and the folk dances of different parts of India, and studied contemporary dance, ballet and TaiChi, and choreography at the London Contemporary Dance School. He studied Capoeira at the London School of Capoeira and African Dance.

He is director of the Attakalari Centre for Movement Arts and Services, Bangalore, formed by artists from different disciplines to facilitate the development of a South Asian dance idiom. He has to his credit several choreographic works including "Parabolas", "Jyroscape", "Beyond the Walls for Men", "City Maps", "Scanned", and "Trans Avatar".

2 and 3
Sequences from "Trans Avatar",
choreographed by
Jayachandran Palazhy and
produced by the Imlata Dance
Company (UK) in partnership
with Attakalari and Neues
Theatre, Munich. It is a
multimedia performance
incorporating contemporary
dance, martial arts, and
integrated sound and digital
technology. It explores multiple
identities of individuals and
manifestations in different
physical and mental spaces.
Photographs: Allan F. Parker.

1
"Fragility, Three Solos" by
Padmini Chettur, explores
demystification and the need
to speak a physical language
that needs no tradition.
Photograph: G. Venket Ram.

Padmini Chettur has worked with Chandralekha and performed in her major choreographic works. She has emerged as an independent choreographer creating original works with the Padmini Chettur Group, Chennai.

2
Another sequence from
"Fragility". Photograph:
Claudia Esch-Kenkel.

Maya Krishna Rao is known for her creation of solo dance theatre pieces which draw inspiration from Kathakali. Since her childhood she was trained in this dance form by renowned teachers. Maya is based in New Delhi and was an Associate Professor at the National School of Drama. Her pieces have also been performed at theatre festivals overseas.

In her choreography of "Khol Do", based on the short story by Saadat Hasan Manto, Maya uses Kathakali technique to the music of Phillip Glass. "Khol Do" is set during the riots at the time of partition, in which a father searches for his daughter lost in the crowds of fleeing people on a railway platform.

1
In "Khol Do", Maya Krishna
Rao portrays the anguish of
the father; the father becomes
his daughter through
movement, and finds her in
himself and in dance.
Photograph courtesy
Maya Krishna Rao.

Gitanjali Kolanad has been involved in the practice, performance, and teaching of Bharata Natyam for over thirty years. She received training in Bharata Natyam at Kalakshetra, and also from C.V. Chandrasekhar, the late Nana Kasar, and Kalanidhi Narayanan. Her contemporary choreography develops from this foundation, using the traditional form and technique of Bharata Natyam to explore contemporary ideas and aesthetics. Many of the dance pieces arise from her collaborations with painter M. Natesh, sculptor Valsan Kolleri, poet Judith Kroll, and installation artist Ray Langenback. She is currently based in Toronto.

1
A scene from Gitanjali Kolanad's choreography for "The Seven Deadly Sins of the Petit Bourgeoisie" by Bertolt Brecht and Kurt Weill. The dancers are Gitanjali Kolanad, C.A. Joy, and Pasupati. The production used video installations, varied music (jazz, Carnatic classical, and Tamil film songs), and the spoken word (Tamil and English), together with dance in a cabaret setting. Photograph: Mohandas V. Badgara.

2
Gitanjali in "Walking Naked", 1996. Photograph: Ashok Charles.

196

3
The brass puppet from "Walking Naked" is worn on the shoulders, like the Theyyam masks; with a fine paper covering which is burned, it represents the final dissolution of self for Mahadevi Akka, as she achieves union with Shiva. Photograph: Peter Bregg/ Maclean's.

Trained in Kathak in the Jaipur gharana under Kundanlal Gangani and in the Lucknow gharana under Birju Maharaj and other traditional gurus, **Shovana Narayan**, based in New Delhi, has attempted East-West fusion, exploring the common elements of footwork, rhythm, energy, and salient features of classical Kathak and Spanish Flamenco.

1
Shovana Narayan performing with Spanish Flamenco dancer Dario Arboleda and ballet dancer Christian Rovny, a soloist of the Vienna State Opera. They have toured within India and abroad, setting a trend for similar ventures. Photograph: Ashwani Chopra, courtesy Shovana Narayan.

1
A sequence from "Ka-Tap!"
featuring Samir Chatterjee
(tabla), Neil Applebaum (tap),
Janaki Patrik (Kathak), and
Olivia Rosenkrantz (tap).
Photograph: Frank Gimpaya,
courtesy The Kathak Ensemble.

Janaki Patrik, an American dancer based in New York, was trained in Kathak by Birju Maharaj. She has choreographed "Ka-Tap!", also known as "NewYorkDelhi Mix" with four to twelve dancers and eight to ten musicians. American tap dance joins in a dialogue with Indian Kathak dance, and jazz responds to Hindustani music, using improvisational and melodic structures common to these forms. The dancers and musicians create bridges between American and Indian music and dance forms.

New York-based **Rajika Puri,** trained in Bharata Natyam and Odissi, collaborates with Spanish Flamenco dancer La Conja in Flamenco Natyam, revelling in the synergy generated by Bharata Natyam and Flamenco. Several exponents both in India and abroad have been choreographing fusion experimentations with different dance traditions from different cultural backgrounds, exploring common meeting points.

1
In "Flamenco Natyam", Rajika Puri and La Conja both dance and sing as they explore similarities and differences – in rhythm and footwork, melody and arm movement, sung lyrics and ways of conveying poetic ideas. Photograph: Tejbir Singh.

Indian dancers have been collaborating in joint dance productions with dancers from abroad. Of late there have been several successful intercultural experiments. In "Cendrillon Ailleurs", based on the story of Cinderella, French choreographer **Annette Leday** has collaborated with two male Kathakali dancers who play female roles using Kathakali and modern dance technique.

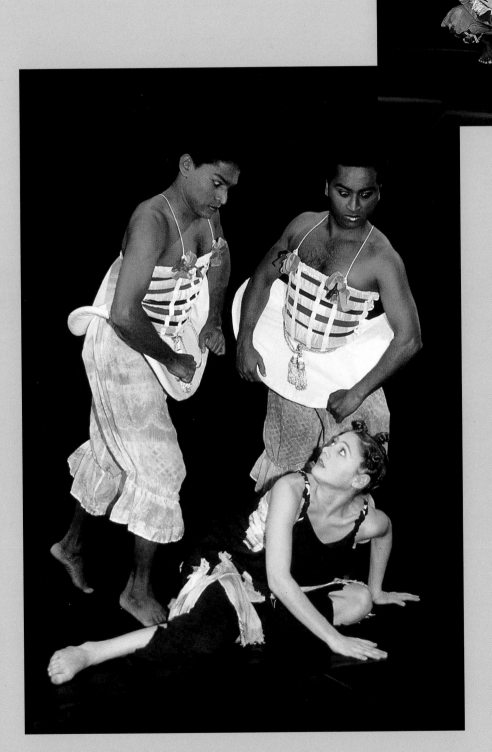

1 and 2
"Cendrillon Ailleurs",
choreographed by Annette
Leday. Photographs courtesy
Annette Leday.

index

Page numbers in *italics* indicate captions/figures

Aarti Dance Company, Thiruvananthapuram 101, 183
Abhinavagupta 13
Ackerman, Belinda 161
Action Players, Kolkata 129–30
Akademi (former Academy of Indian Dance), London 167, 190
Anarta Academy of Kathak, Ahmedabad 182
Angika, London 164
Applebaum, Neil *199*
Arangham Dance Theatre, Chennai 186, *186*
Arboleda, Dario 198
Attakalari Centre for Movement Arts and Services, Bangalore 192, *193*

Bach's Cello Suites 98
Badejo, Peter 178, *179*
Bagouet, Dominique 12
Balasaraswati *14*
Banks, Louis 126
Bannerman, Christopher 164
Bardhan, Shanti 12, *24–25*, 26, 27
Bates, Django 161
Batliboi, Ratan J. 123, 124
Bausch, Pina 123
Bedi, Protima 98
Bejart, Maurice 106
Bel, Andreine 12
Bhabha, Jamshed 12
Bhagwan 136
Bhagyachandra, Raja 70
Bhansali, Sanjay Leela 144
Bharata Natyam 10, 11, 13, *13–15*, 16, 18, 23, 25, 40, 44–46, 48, 49, *50*, 57, 82, 87, 104, 106, 112, 130, *135*, 146–55, *146–51*, 158, 163, 164, 167, *167*, 183, 186, *187*, 190, 192, 196, 200; fusion with Flamenco 200, *200*
Bhaskaracharya *50*
Bhatt, Sujata 103
Bhatta Nayaka 45
Bhattacharya, Debipada 87
Bhavalkar, Uday 126
Bhide, Sucheta 12
Bhojwani, Suresh 123
Bhoomika Creative Dance Centre, New Delhi 11, *26*, 188
Bilasini Devi 73
Binodini Devi, Raj Kumari 75, 78
Birju Maharaj, Pandit 26, 94, *157*, 180, 198, 199
Biswas, Debabrata 87
Biswas, Sharmila 189, *189*
Bombshell, Ursula 163
Bose, Madhu *132*, 136
Bose, Nandalal 33, 34
Bose, Sadhana *132, 134*
Bose, Subhas Chandra 34
Bowers, Faubian 174
Brecht, Bertolt *196*
British Council 104
Brook, Peter 178

Cama, Rohinton 110
Carlson, Carolyn 106
Cerroni, Patrizia 12
Chadha, Sheeba 99
Chakravorty, Sudarshan 177
Chandrabhaga Devi, Srimati U.K. 147
Chandralekha 11–13, 16, 50–58, *50, 53–57*, 112, 190
Chandrasekhar, C.V. 196

Chaoba, Khwairakpam 78
Chatterjea, Ananya *154, 155*
Chatterjee, Samir *199*
Chettur, Padmini 194, *194*
Chhau 25, 30, *30*, 34, 40, 42, 90, 94, 97, 104, 161, *180*, 190, *190*
Cholom 70, 73
Chopra, Yash 138
Chuma, Yoshiko 190
Chundee, Sheena *167*
Citaristi, Ileana 12, 190, *190*
Clark School for the Deaf, Chennai 130
Clyne, Nada *171*
(The) Collective Dance Theatre, New York 87
Coomaraswamy, Ananda 44, 174
Coorlawala, Uttara Asha 12, 17, 18, 106–17, *106, 111, 112, 114, 115*, 120, *168, 171–75*
Cowton, Andy 164
Cuni, Amelia 126
Cunningham, Merce 106, 164

Daksha Sheth Dance Company 102
Dancers' Guild, Kolkata 82, 85, 86, 91
Dartington Hall, Devon 33, 89, 156
Davar, Shiamak 142, 143
Davis, Gary 168
Deboo, Astad *4*, 12, 18, 118–30, *118, 120, 122, 123, 125, 127–29*
DeLavallade, Carmen 12
Desai, Atul *11*, 62
Devissaro 94, 97, 98, 101, 102
Dhananjayan, V.P. and Shanta 192
Dhareshwar, Vivek 144
Dixit, Madhuri 132, *139, 141*, 144
Doordarshan 155
Dove, Simon 99
Drishtikon Dance Foundation, New Delhi 180
Dubey, Satyadev 123, 126
Dunning, Jennifer 110, 113

East-West Dance Encounter, Mumbai/Delhi 11, 12, 16, 106
Elephanta Dance Festival, Mumbai 121
Emberton, Gwyn 164
Erdman, Joan 171, 176

Faiz Ahmed Faiz *154*
Fitkin, Graham 161
Flatischer, Reinhart 126
Fokine, Michel 152
Fried, Jodie 178

Gangani, Kundanlal 198
Gaston, Anne Marie 12
Ghai, Subhash 144, 145
Ghosh, Santidev 34
Glass, Phillip 94, 195
Gonzagiana Jr., Louis 126
Gopi Krishna 136, *139*
Gopinath 21
Gopinath, Madhu *100, 101, 105*, 183, *183–85*
Graham, Martha 90, 91, 106, *106*, 112, 120
Gundecha Brothers 125–27

Hameenniemi, Eero 104
Hammel, Peter 126
Haren Ghosh Impresario, Calcutta 75
Haydon, Mark and Philipe 178
Helen 132, *144*
Hema Malini 132
Hirst, Damien 123
Hula Group, Imphal 127

Ilayaraaja 161
Imlata Dance Company, UK *193*
Indian Council for Cultural Relations 11
Indian National Theatre, Bombay 25
Indira Gandhi National Centre for the Arts, New Delhi 98
Ironbiter, Suzanne 178

Jagoi 71
Jarrett, Keith 98
Jawaharlal Nehru Manipur Dance Academy, Imphal 75
Jayant, Ananda Shankar 177
Jeyasingh, Shobana 18, 157, 158, 160, 161, *161*, 163, *163*, 164, 167
Jhaveri Sisters 71, 112
Jhaveri, Sushilbhai 112
Johar, Navtej Singh 190, *191*
Jones, Bill T. 190
Joss, Kurt 34, 89
Joy, C.A. *196*

Kalakshetra, Chennai 10, 192, 196
Kalanidhi, Toronto 16
Kalaripayattu 13, 31, 40, 42, *53*, 58, 90, 98, 101, 105, 162, 183, 192
Kalidasa *46*, 48
Kalyanpurkar, Mohanrao *172*
Kamaljeet 99
Kant, Ratnabali *177*
Kapoor, Anil 142
Kapoor, Karisma 144
Kapoor, Raj 138
Karthika, R. 130
Kasar, Nana 196
Kashyap, Tripura *177*
Kathak 10, *11*, 16, *16*, 18, 23, 25, 26, 40, 60–69, *61, 63, 67*, 94, 98, 99, 104, 120, 139, *139*, 152, *157,159*, 163, 167, 180, *180*, 182, *182*, 198, 199; fusion with Flamenco 152, 198, *198*; fusion with tap dance and jazz 199, *199*
Kathakali 10, *17*, 18, 25, 26, 34, 40, 45, *45*, 46, 48, 49, *49*, 82, *120*, 122, 123, 186, 192, 195, 201
Kerala Kala Mandalam, Cheruturuthi 10, *16, 17*, 34
Khajuraho Dance Festival 126
Khan, Akram 18, 157, *157–60*, 163–64, 167
Khan, Farah 139
Khan, Keith 163, 167
Khan, Nusrat Fateh Ali *154*
Khan, Saroj 139, *140, 141*
Khan, Shahrukh 132, 142
Khandwani, Sudha 16
Khokar, Ashish 176
Khokar, Mohan 176
Khoo, Mavin 18, *160*, 164, *165, 167*
Kolanad, Gitanjali 196, *196–97*
Kolleri, Valsan 196
(The) Kosh, London *97*, 104, 183
Kothari, Sunil 176
Kripalani, Nandita 36
Krishan, Hari *150*
Krishna Iyer, E. *13*
Krishna Rao, Maya 195, *195*
Krishna Rao, U.S. 147
Krishnamurthy, Yamini 12
Kroll, Judith 196
Kshemavathy, Kalamandalam 192
Kuchipudi 11, 26
Kumar, Anil *100, 103*
Kumar, Atul 99
Kumar, Krishna 136
Kumar, Surya 136
Kunju Kurup, Guru 45

La Conja 200, *200*
La Meri 174
La Troupe Kala Bharati, Montreal *146, 148*, 155
Laban, Rudolf 34, 89
Lai Haraoba 41, 70, 78
Lakhia, Kumudini *11*, 12, 16, 17, 60–69, *61, 67, 69*, 94, 180, 182
Lalit Kala Akademi, New Delhi 10, 133
Lalvani, Haresh 111
Langenback, Ray 196
Lechner, Georg 11, 16, 106, 168
Leday, Annette 201, *201*
Lightfoot, Louise 73
Lilly, Janet 190

Linke, Susanne   12
Long, Stephen   12
Louis, Murray   118
Lowen, Sharon   12

Macdonald, Alistair   161
Madame Menaka   10, *16*, 21
Mahapatra, Guru Kelucharan   26, 189, 190
mallkhamb   *103*, 183
Mangaldas, Aditi   180, *180*, *181*
Manipuri   10, 18, 23, 25, 34, 35, 40, 41, 70–81, *71–81*,
    87, 123, *127*, *132*, *134*, *138*
Mansingh, Sonal   12
Manto, Saadat Hasan   195
Manuel, Peter   134
Matondkar, Urmila   139
Mauger, Elizabeth   12
Max Mueller Bhavan, Mumbai and Delhi   11, 16, 106,
    123
McCarthy, Justin   190
Meduri, Avanthi   12
Mehta, Ved   98
Menon, Narayana   12
Menon, Sadanand   12, 176
Merchant, Vaibhavi   *4*, *142*
Messiaen, Olivier   106
Michael, Moya   164
Mohini Attam   11, 34, 186
Morris, Madeleine   163
MTV   138, 139
Mudgal, Shubha   126
Mylapore Gowri Amma   *14*, *15*

Naik, Krishna Chandra   94
Nair, Santosh   177, *180*
Namboodripad, Guru   23
Nandikeshwara   13
Narain, Brij   120–21
Narayan, Shovana   198, *198*
Narayanan, Kalanidhi   86, 196
Nataraj-Heri, Madhu   177
Natasankirtan   78
Natesh, M.   196
National Centre for the Performing Arts (NCPA), Mumbai
    11, 12
National Gallery of Modern Art, Mumbai   124
Natyashastra of Bharata   16, 45, *50*, 91, 174
Natyashram, Thiruvananthapuram   101
Navanritya   18, 40, *42*, 82–92, 106
Nehru, Jawaharlal   27
Neues Theatre, Munich   *193*
Niranjana, Tejaswini   144
Niyogi-Nakra, Mamata   18
Nordi, Cleo   *15*
Nritya Seva Mandali, Vrindaban   98
Nrityagram, Bangalore   98
Nrityalayam, Khandala   10
Nupi Khubak Ishei   70
Nyman, Michael   158, 161

Odissi   11, 23, 26, 40, 87, *154*, 167, 189, 200
Odissi Vision and Movement Centre, Kolkata   189
Omkarnath Thakur, Pandit   62

Pada, Lata   *151*, *153*
Padmini   136
Palazhy, Jayachandran   192, *192*, *193*
Panicker, Chathunni   *45*
Pannicker, Guru E.K.   122
Parekh, Asha   136
Parikh, Ishira   182
Pasupati   *196*
Patel, Dashrath   12
Patel, Priti   *77*, 78, *78–81*
Patrik, Janaki   199, *199*
Pavlova, Anna   *10*, *15*, 16, 20, *21*, 156
Pawar, Pratap   *157*
Perrin, Glynn   161
Phalke, Dadasaheb   133

Pillai, Guru Ellappa   45, 50
Pillai, Guru Kandappa   23
Pillai, Guru Kitappa   45, *150*
Pillai, Guru Meenakshisundaram   *15*, 44
Pillai, Guru Muthukumaran   45
Pink Floyd   123
Plisseskaia, Maia   122
Pong Chalam Dancers of Manipur   123
Prabhudeva   132, 144
Prahlad Das, Guru   120
Priyagopalasana, Rajkumar   73, 75
Pudumjee, Dadi   *122*, 123, 127
Punja, Shobita   *186*
Puri, Rajika   *149*, 200, *200*

Rabindra Bharati University, Kolkata   16
Rabindra Sangeet   35
Raghavan, V.   176
Ragini Devi   21, 174
Rai, Aishwarya   132
Rai, Amit   133
Raj, P.L.   136, 143
Ram Gopal   12, 60, 147, 156, 167
Ramamani, R.A.   161
Ranga Rao, V.A.K.   133, 136
Rasalila   70, 78, *78*, 81, *134*
Ratnam, Anita   186, *186–87*
Ravel, Maurice   *175*
Ray, Shamita   *163*
Rekha   132, *140*, *145*
Rehman, Waheeda   132, 136
Reshma   *155*
Ritha Devi   12
Rosenkrantz, Olivia   199
Rovny, Christian   198
Roy, Sanjoy   18
Rukmini Devi   10, *14*, *15*, 21, 174

Sachin Shankar Ballet Unit, Mumbai   25, *31*
Sahitya Akademi, New Delhi   10, 133
Sajeev, Vikom   *105*, 183, *183–85*
Sampradaya Dance Creations, Mississauga   *153*
Samson, Leela   190
Samudra Centre for Indian Contemporary Performing
    Arts, Thiruvananthapuram   183
Sandhya   *139*
Sangeet Natak Akademi, New Delhi   10, 27, 75, 133,
    177
Sankalpam, UK   164
Santiniketan (Viswabharati) 10, *12*, 20, 32–34, 47, 71, 89
Sarabhai, Mallika   *4*, 12, *46*, *48*, 178, *178*, *179*
Sarabhai, Mrinalini   12, 17, 25, *36*, 44–58, *45*, *46*, *48*,
    49, 178
Sattriya   11
Sawhney, Nitin   163
Saxena, S.K.   176
Saxena, Sarveshwar Dayal   65
Schaffer, Pierre   106
Schmidt, Jochen   12
Serbjeet Singh, Shanta   12, 112, 176
Seshagopalan, Madurai T.N.   154
Sethi, Rajeev   97
Shah, Maulik   182, *182*
Shah, Ranvir   186
Shambhu Maharaj, Guru   60
Shanbag, Sunil   120–21, 123
Shankar, Anand   *175*
Shankar, Uday   10, *10*, 11, 12, 17, 20–31, *21–24*, *31*, 71,
    89, 136, *137*, 156, 177
Shantaram, V.   *139*
Sharma, Bharat   12, *30*, 177
Sharma, Kalyanji Prasad   98
Sharma, Narendra   *4*, 11, *26*, *28–30*, 188
Sharma, Sangeeta   188, *188*
Sharvani, Isha   *100*, 102, *103*, 105
Sheth, Daksha   16, 18, 94–105, *95–105*, 183
Shri Hari   190
Shriram Bharatiya Kala Kendra, New Delhi   25–26
Sija, Charu   *71*, 73, *73*, 75

Silkstone, Francis   126
Singh, Babu   75, 78
Singh, Dayanita   *140*
Singh, Guru Amubi   23, 71
Singh, Guru Bipin   71, 78
Singh, Guru Devabrata   127
Singh, Guru Nabhakumar   20, 71
Singh, Laishram Somorendra   78
Singh, Th. Chaotombi   75, *75*
Singh, Th. Tarunkumar   73, 75
Singh, W. Lokendrajit   75
Singh, Vishwakant   94
Singhjit Singh, R.K.   25, 71, *71–73*, *73*, 75
Sircar, Manjusri Chaki   18, 32–43, *39*, *41*, *42*, 82–85,
    82, 87, 89
Sircar, Ranjabati   18, 82–92, *82–90*
Sivamani   126
Sparling, Peter   190
Srivastava, Rahul   142, 145
St Denis, Ruth   20, 115, 174
Stemerding, Ad and Han   110, 111
Studio Abhyas, New Delhi   190
Subramaniam, Arundhathi   18
Subuddu   176
Sullivan, Timothy   *153*
Sun Ock Lee   *175*
Sundaram, Chitra   12
Sunder Prasad, Pandit   60
Sussman, Stanley B.   *174*
Swaminathan, Ammu   46

Tagore, Protima   33, 34, 89
Tagore, Rabindranath   10, *12*, 18, 20, 21, 32–43, *33*, *36*,
    47, *48*, 71, 87, 89
Tangente, Montreal   154
Tao   102
Taylor, Mark   *187*
Thakkar, Rasesh   16
Thang-ta   18, 31, 42, 70, 73, 78, *78*, *81*, 90, 127
Thapar, Romila   112
Thaper, Mini   *180*
Theyyam   *197*
Thomas, Rosie   133
Triveni Kala Sangam, New Delhi   25, 71, 73

Uday Shankar India Culture Centre, Almora   10, 23–24,
    26, 71

Vajifdar, Shirin   12
Vallathol Narayana Menon   10, *16*, 174
van Schulenburch, Ellen   102
Vasan, S.S.   *135*
Vasudevan, Preeti   *149*
Vatsyayan, Kapila   17, 112, 176
Vempati Chinna Satyam, Guru   26
Venkataraman, Leela   176
Vivaldi's *Four Seasons*   94
Vivarta Dance Festival, London   99, 102
Volans, Kevin   161
von Tiedemann, Cylla   *153*
Vyjayanthimala   136, 143

Wakhevitch, Igor   12, 106, 110
Warren, Vincent   153
Weill, Kurt   *196*
Wigman, Mary   34, 89
Wuppertal Dance Company, Germany   123

Yakshagana   40
yoga   13, 106, 111, 112, *112*, *180*, 182
YUVA Company, London   102

Zacharia, Paul   101
Zakir Hussain   126
Zarilli, Phillip   176

contributors

Kapila Vatsyayan is an internationally renowned scholar, an authority on Indian classical and folk dances, and author of several books on Indian art, which have been path-breaking in terms of their interdisciplinary approach. She combines both practical and theoretical knowledge of dance, and her magnum opus *Classical Indian Dance* has set very high standards of scholarship in the subject. Several honours have been bestowed upon her. She was Secretary, Department of Arts, Ministry of Culture, Government of India and is responsible for the unified vision of the Indira Gandhi National Centre for the Arts, New Delhi of which she was Academic Director.

Manjusri Chaki Sircar was inspired by her readings of Tagore to develop ideas on her dance style and methodology outside the boundaries of classical doctrine. Trained in Bharata Natyam, Odissi, and Manipuri by the reputed gurus, she and her daughter Ranjabati evolved a methodology of Navanritya. On her return to Kolkata from the USA in 1980, she established Dancers' Guild and choreographed works which addressed issues such as threats to the environment, horrors of war, social repression, and the subjugation of women. She passed away in 2000.

Mrinalini Sarabhai received training in Bharata Natyam from the great gurus like Meenakshisundaram Pillai and in Kathakali from Kunju Kurup. Founder of Darpana Dance Academy, Ahmedabad, she has choreographed several works within the traditional format and extended the language of dance with innovations and thematic content, reflecting contemporary issues with great success. Spanning a dance career of more than six decades, her interests range from dance, the environment, handicrafts, and culture to social work.

Chandralekha is central in the Indian dance context for boldly interrogating the classical heritage, historicizing it, and restating it in contemporary terms. The cumulative direction of her search was to return to the basics of the body and its energies within changing time/space dynamics. Her work is the yardstick by which new and contemporary dance from India is measured. She lived in Chennai and passed away in 2006.

Kumudini Lakhia was trained in Kathak by the legendary gurus Shambhu Maharaj and Pandit Sunder Prasad. At an early age she was invited by Ram Gopal to join his company. She toured the world with him and gained invaluable experience watching the best of dancers from all parts of the world. Settled in Ahmedabad she established her Kadamb School of Music and has choreographed brilliant works in Kathak extending the boundaries of Kathak with contemporary sensibilities.

Ranjabati Sircar was the principal dancer and associate choreographer of Dancers' Guild, Kolkata, besides being a soloist of classical and contemporary dance forms. Her seminal article reproduced in this volume explains the basic concept of Navanritya. Her untimely death in 1999 robbed the Indian contemporary dance scene of a gifted young dancer and choreographer.

Daksha Sheth, trained by Kumudini Lakhia and Birju Maharaj in Kathak, further studied Mayurbhanj Chhau and later on Kalaripayattu to expand her dance language. While based in Thiruvananthapuram, Daksha Sheth with her husband Devissaro's support choreographed several works. Her daughter Isha Sharvani and son Tao also perform in the Daksha Sheth Dance Company. Daksha has also collaborated with the British Dance Company and choreographed a staggeringly wide range of solo numbers.

Uttara Asha Coorlawala, Adjunct Professor, Alvin Ailey Dance at Fordham University, New York, is a pioneer in Modern Dance in India. She was trained by Martha Graham, Pearl Lang, Merce Cunningham, and others in New York. She has also studied Bharata Natyam, Kathak, and Odissi. She has attempted fusion of dance forms. For her seminal work, "Classical and Contemporary Indian Dance", she received a Ph.D. from New York University. She divides her time between India and New York.

Astad Deboo studied traditional Kathakali and Kathak and evolved his own individual style from the varied influences of world cultures over the last three decades. Diverse influences have given him the rich vocabulary of a successful soloist and the resources to engage in creative collaborations with performers in other disciplines, from music, martial art of Manipur, drummers of Manipur, and puppetry. For the last 22 years he has been working with the deaf and street children. His work has opened doors for the present generation of dancers to venture into contemporary choreography. He has received the Padma Shri and the Sangeet Natak Akademi award.

Arundhathi Subramaniam is a poet and critic and writes on various aspects of Indian culture with a broad perspective and commendable insight, bringing to her writings a freshness of approach and sharp observation. She is based in Mumbai and organizes special programmes for the National Centre for the Performing Arts.

Mamata Niyogi-Nakra studied Bharata Natyam under U.S. Krishna Rao. She is a leading choreographer, and founder-director of Kala Bharati, Montreal, an institution training students in Bharata Natyam. She is recognized as a pioneer in presenting Bharata Natyam in group formations and is widely respected for her academic interest in Indian classical dance. She has served on many committees on music and dance in Canada.

Sanjoy Roy is a writer, editor, critic, and designer based in London. He has written for *The Guardian, Dance Now, Dancing Times, Dance Theatre Journal, Dance Europe, Pulse,* and *Tanssi* (Finland), as well as programme notes for several dance companies. He was editor of *Dance Now* and *extrADiTion* magazines. He is the author of "Contemporary Indian Dance in the Western City" in *Dance in the City* edited by Helen Thomas (1997). He has won several design awards.